BLOODAXE CONTEMPORARY FRENCH POETS

Throughout the twentieth century, France has been a dominant force in the development of European culture. It has made essential contributions and advances not just in literature but in all the arts, from the novel to film and philosophy; in drama (Theatre of the Absurd), art (Cubism and Surrealism) and literary theory (Structuralism and Post-Structuralism). These very different art forms and intellectual modes find a dynamic meeting-point in post-war French poetry.

Some French poets are absorbed by the latest developments in philosophy or psychoanalysis. Others explore relations between poetry and painting, between the written word and the visual image. There are some whose poetry is rooted in Catholicism, and others who have remained faithful to Surrealism, and whose poetry is bound to a life of action or political commitment.

Because it shows contemporary French poetry in a broader context, this new series will appeal both to poetry readers and to anyone with an interest in French culture and intellectual life. The books themselves also provide an imaginative and exciting approach to French poets which makes them ideal study texts for schools, colleges and universities.

Each volume is a single, unabridged collection of poems presented in a parallel-text format, with the French text facing an English verse translation by a distinguished expert or poet-translator. The editor of each book is an authority on the particular writer, and in each case the editor's introduction presents not only a critical appreciation of the work and its place in the author's output but also a comprehensive account of its social, intellectual and cultural background.

The series itself has been planned in such a way that the individual volumes will build up into a stimulating and informative introduction to contemporary French poetry, giving readers both an intimate experience of how French poets think and write, and a working overview of what makes poetry important in France. It is launched with three works by some of the best-known French poets of the post-war period: Yves Bonnefoy, René Char and Henri Michaux.

BLOODAXE CONTEMPORARY FRENCH POETS

Series Editors: Timothy Mathews & Michael Worton

Timothy Mathews is Fellow in French at Trinity Hall, Cambridge. He has published *Reading Apollinaire: Theories of Poetic Language* (Manchester University Press, 1987), and is now writing a book for Cambridge University Press on alienation in modern French literature and painting. The first volume in the Bloodaxe Contemporary French Poets series, *On the Motion and Immobility of Douve* by Yves Bonnefoy, has an introduction by Timothy Mathews.

Michael Worton is Senior Lecturer in French at University College London. He has published extensively on contemporary French writers, co-edited *Intertextuality: Theories and Practices* (Manchester University Press, 1990), and is now writing books on Samuel Beckett and Michel Tournier. The second volume in the Bloodaxe Contemporary French Poets series, *The Dawn Breakers* by René Char, is edited and translated by Michael Worton.

For further details of the Bloodaxe Contemporary French Poets series, please see pages 157-58 of this book.

BLOODAXE CONTEMPORARY FRENCH POETS: 1

YVES BONNEFOY

On the Motion and Immobility of Douve

Du mouvement et de l'immobilité de Douve

Translated by
GALWAY KINNELL

Introduction by
TIMOTHY MATHEWS

BLOODAXE BOOKS

BLOODAXE CONTEMPORARY FRENCH POETS: 1
Yves Bonnefoy: *On the Motion and Immobility of Douve*

Original French text of *Du mouvement et de l'immobilité de Douve*
by Yves Bonnefoy © Mercure de France 1953.
English translation © Galway Kinnell 1960, 1961, 1962, 1964 and
© *Poetry* (Chicago) 1964, reprinted by kind permission of Ohio
University Press from *On the Motion and Immobility of Douve* (1968).
Introduction © Timothy Mathews 1992.

ISBN: 1 85224 132 2

This edition published 1992 by
Bloodaxe Books Ltd,
P.O. Box 1SN,
Newcastle upon Tyne NE99 1SN.

Bloodaxe Books Ltd acknowledges
the financial assistance of Northern Arts.

Bloodaxe Books Ltd and Timothy Mathews wish
to thank the Department of French, the University of Cambridge
for help given towards the costs of this book.

Cover reproduction by V & H Reprographics, Newcastle upon Tyne.

Cover printing by J. Thomson Colour Printers Ltd, Glasgow.

Printed in Great Britain by
The Alden Press, Osney Mead, Oxford.

CONTENTS

Du mouvement et de l'immobilité de Douve

On the Motion and Immobility of Douve

GENERAL EDITORS' PREFACE

The Bloodaxe Contemporary French Poets series aims to bring a broad range of post-war French poetry to as wide an English-speaking readership as possible, and it has specific features which are designed to further this aim.

First of all, each volume is devoted to a complete, unabridged work by a poet. This is designed to maintain the coherence of what a poet is trying to achieve in publishing a book of poems. We hope that in this way, the particular sense of a poet working within language will be highlighted. Secondly, each work appears in parallel translation. Finally, each work is prefaced by a substantial essay which gives a critical appreciation of the book of poetry, of its place in its author's work, as well as an account of its social and intellectual context.

In each case, this essay is written by an established critic with a love of French poetry. It aims not only to be informative, but also to respond in a lively and distinctive way to the pleasures and challenges of reading each poet. Similarly, the translators, often poets in their own right, adopt a range of different approaches, and in every case they seek out an English that gives voice to the uniqueness of the French poems.

Each translation in the series is not just faithful to the original, but aims to recreate the poet's voice or its nearest equivalent in another language: each is a translation from French poetry into English poetry. Each essay seeks to make its own statement about how and why we read poetry and think poetry. The work of each poet dovetails with others in the series to produce a living illustration of the importance of poetry in contemporary French culture.

INTRODUCTION

Overture

Born in 1923, Yves Bonnefoy is currently Professor of Comparative
Studies and of the Poetic Function at the Collège de France in
Paris. His writing brings together some of the major trends of
artistic enquiry in post-war France. It is particularly appropriate
that *Du mouvement et de l'immobilité de Douve*, Bonnefoy's first
full-scale volume of poetry, should be published as the first book
in the Bloodaxe Contemporary French Poets series, for this series
is devoted to bringing recent French poetry to a wider English-
speaking readership, and Bonnefoy himself has had a lifelong fas-
cination with the problems of translation, particularly with render-
ing Shakespeare and Yeats into French.

In Bonnefoy's case, this does not involve any simple attempt to
popularise or to provide approximative renditions. His point of
departure here is the fear that all that might remain in a French
translation of *King Lear*, for example, is a disembodied Shakespeare.
For language, in Bonnefoy's account of it, is precisely a visceral,
intensely material element in our existence. This perception forms
the basis of Bonnefoy's broad investigation into the aspirations of
poetry and of its range. His anxiety concerns the essentially abstract
quality of words, and the ways in which this distorts the immediate,
material quality of our contact with the world. This concern with
what separates words from some essential truth hidden in objects
involves Bonnefoy in wide-ranging investigations of the spiritual
and of the sacred, which take in philosophical as well as theological
thought.

But for all Bonnefoy's intellectual drive and rigour, his poetry
is essentially of the concrete and the tangible. It addresses itself to
our most familiar and intimate experiences of objects and of each
other. In an age permeated by notions of fragmentation and alien-
ation, Bonnefoy's writing stands out for the way it strives to wipe
language clean and to take us beyond what in many ways he pre-
sents as an essential fault in language.

Yet even to speak of language as a general idea, or as a dominant
experience in itself, may already strike English-speaking readers as
antagonistic to the particular pleasures of poetry. We may find that
the familiar, the intimate, the tangible are all qualities which are
ill-served by writers preoccupied by the implications of writing

itself. But here we run up against a seemingly ingrained set of cross-Channel misreadings. An enmeshing of great intellectual concerns with an exploration of emotional life for which we turn to poetry is a spontaneous feature of English verse from Shakespeare, Donne, and Milton, to Wordsworth, Coleridge and Gerard Manley Hopkins. But it has become strange to us, even unacceptable at times, to think of Victor Hugo, for example, combining metaphysical speculation with an intense involvement with the major social upheavals of nineteenth-century France. We may be alienated by the philosophical investigations of syntax and semantics engaged in by Mallarmé; or astonished at Rimbaud's textual battles with the weight of history and of precedence. We may look askance at attempts by the Surrealists to have all the arts address experiences of the unconscious, and to have them engage in ideological struggle as well. And yet all these figures, along with Baudelaire and Apollinaire, form a living cluster of experiences, of writing and thinking, that is part of the culture with which modern French poetry interacts.

Bonnefoy himself is engaged in a continuing search for a genuine integration of the material and the spiritual elements in our experience, the temporal and the permanent ones. This takes the form not only of writing poetry but also of his extremely wide-ranging work as an essayist on the arts. Objects of his meditation include Byzantine art, Quattrocento art, Italian Renaissance art, the painting of Claude Lorrain and of Nicholas Poussin, the Baroque, French poetry from François Villon to the present, the interpretation and translation of Shakespeare and of Yeats, and many contemporary painters, such as Raoul Ubac and particularly Alberto Giacometti. The sheer breadth and the variety of Bonnefoy's investigation bear witness to a belief that our intellectual and emotional lives are not to be compartmentalised. Equally, this varied investigation emphasises the provisional, mobile, provocative ways in which ideas are made present in Bonnefoy's writing. Readers of English or American poetry may want to think of Bonnefoy's poetry in comparison with the working, living symbolism of Yeats; or with the deft confusing of the abstract and the intensely concrete in the writing of Wallace Stevens – who once pronounced that 'the theory of poetry is the theory of life'.

Inaugural

In 1981, with many of his major books of poetry and essays behind him, Yves Bonnefoy took his chair at the Collège de France. This chair that had been inaugurated to replace the one occupied by Roland Barthes until his death. Despite the spectacular arbitrariness of Barthes's death – he was hit by a truck in the Latin Quarter – this institutional juxtaposition seems to evoke the specific quality of Bonnefoy's vocation and commitment. More than a juxtaposition, this passage might rather suggest an opposition, an intellectual about-turn within a seat of intellectual endeavour that in the period since the events in Paris of 1968 has housed such thinkers as Claude Lévi-Strauss and Michel Foucault. Along with Lacan, Derrida and Barthes himself, these figures have done as much as anyone in contemporary France to promote anxiety about our investment in certain notions we seem bound to hold dear: notions such as individuality in its uniqueness, subjectivity in its intimacy, creativity in its primacy. And yet these seem to be the very notions Bonnefoy bears allegiance to in his own inaugural lecture, which was entitled *La Présence et l'image/Presence and Image*. It is a complex, challenging and in many ways moving account of our desire, and indeed our capacity, to say 'I'.

Barthes's chair was a chair of semiology, a 'science of signs' forming a branch of the 'structuralist' pursuit of knowledge that, at least in France, propelled such different disciplines as linguistics, anthropology and psychoanalysis in the 1960s and since. This wide-ranging reappraisal of cultural existence has had particular effects on responses to the arts and on notions of artistic production. Barthes's notorious essay on *The Death of the Author* championed the idea that mastery of expression and thought is an illusion. It is an illusion that confuses our understanding of the multiple conventions which allow experiences to be exchanged and interventions to be constructed. In the wake of such arguments, a belief in the power of authorial intention loses ground to the notion of a network, a 'structure', in terms of which we might chart the ideological, linguistic, and unconscious boundaries that demarcate the intelligible as well as the permissible.

Even now, such notions seem to strike at the heart of what we understand by art, the pleasure and the impetus we receive from it. Already in 1981, the year in which Bonnefoy took up his Chair at the Collège de France, the complacent rationalism implicit in the 'structuralist' approach had become unacceptable. Its inability to deal with how we *identify* with cultural forms, and aesthetic ones in particular, had made it seem asphyxiatingly dry. But Bonnefoy's sense of history is a complex and a generous one. Even though the *post*-structuralist moment was in full swing in 1981, he decided to give an inaugural lecture which would return to that stake which seemed to have been driven into the heart of the creative impetus by *structuralist* rationalism. He did so by making a number of references in his lecture to the inaugural lecture Barthes had himself given at the Collège de France in 1977, which is known as *Leçon/Inaugural Lecture*.

In fact, paradoxically, this is a lecture in which Barthes himself chooses to express disaffection with semiology and the tyrannies it seemed establish. It is precisely Barthes's own estrangement from an overriding methodological concern with language as a system of conventional signs prescribing and proscribing that gives Bonnefoy the encouragement he needs in taking up the reins again himself. The task he sets himself in establishing a chair devoted to examining 'the function of poetry' is no less than to justify commitment to poetry itself and to the inwardness it proclaims.

But he seeks to do so not in *opposition* to critical systems, and the anxiety about self-expression that accompanies them, but in an adventurous *integration* of the two. 'To my mind,' he writes, 'poetry and new criticism are not made to contradict each other for much longer. Soon they might form but a single approach to life.' What is the basis for this confident affirmation? And what is the generosity of poetic giving that we might discover here?

The notion of a 'text' is one that has journeyed from France into Anglo-Saxon parlance with far greater ease than some of its 'new critical' cousins. In schools everywhere we talk of set 'texts', and we easily and usefully talk of 'the text' rather than the novel, play or poem. More generally, we talk of 'sub-texts' in countless varieties of social and cultural interchange. In critical comment of all kinds, 'text' acts as a kind of password into a plural, multi-levelled type of enquiry and awareness. 'Text' is essentially a contribution by Barthes to ways of looking at language as a system of conventions. For Barthes, such systems are more open-ended than we might suppose if we imagined we were fully in control of our language every time we used it. 'Text' suggests an open-ended system of making sense, but nevertheless, on some levels at least, it is also open to being circumscribed.

Bonnefoy returns to the notion of 'text' in his lecture, presenting it as a contemporary concern that must be confronted in affirming poetic craft and aspiration:

Where once used to speak those we called geniuses, believing them to have journeyed directly to superior truths, galaxies have now begun to shine which we call text, more complex and resonant spaces than we were able to formulate in earlier times, but into which we roam vainly amongst constellations and shadows in search of the being who, after all, from within the abyss without top or bottom of the blank page, is the one to have assembled or scattered all these signs.

An evocative account, itself acting poetically to involve us in the mobility of intellectual effects and sensations that are 'text'. And yet, there is a sense that, even in 1981, Bonnefoy is talking of an outdated 'text', one that belongs to what one might call the classical structuralism of the sixties. The problem of text seems at once acknowledged and circumvented. The question is perhaps not so much *who* it is that finds a way through the dimensionless labyrinth comprising signs, precedence and unconscious intention, but *how*. What are the decisions involved, and what are the costs? At the same time, no one more than Bonnefoy seeks to rise to the consequences of this 'textual' shift in the concerns of readers and writers. Assertions of truth and a sense of the world as knowable, give way to a pressure to focus on the extent to which we, as individual sign-users, can direct the impact of signs and understand their force. Bonnefoy identifies a pressure to

analyse states of utterance, signifiers fugitively turned in on unreal signifieds, each catalysing the production of the other, making use of the universe rather than allowing it to be expressed.

Bonnefoy is engaging in a highly allusive way with the linguistic terms *signifier* and *signified*, a coupling which forms one of the mainstays of all 'textual' theory and practice. Coined by the Swiss linguist Ferdinand de Saussure in his seminal *Course in General Linguistics*, the term *signifier* refers to the physical properties of a sign – phonetic, typographical, visual, etc – while *signified* refers to the concept specified by these properties – not the particular word in front of us, but the idea to which you and I are appealing, for example, when we read 'word'. One of the consequences of adopting this dyad is that it focuses attention on the production of sense – the relating of the typographical elements of language to an idea – as a matter of convention. Making sense is no longer thought of as fixing or reaffirming unimpeachable truths or entities of knowledge. To shoulder the conviction that language operates an interplay between signifier and signified is to give up forever the equation, beloved of Plato, of a noun and a definitive name. R.M. Hare in his *Plato* in the Past Masters series (Oxford University Paperbacks) takes the example of a circle, and ponders on the fact that 'if we call anything a circle we are implying that it is a plane figure of a certain sort; and in order to know this we do not have to know any celestial entities'. Bonnefoy takes part in giving up such a metaphysical notion of naming and its potency, perhaps even in grieving for it, in suggesting that contemporary writers seem bound to 'make use of the universe' rather than allowing it to be revealed.

It is in the context of such grieving that Bonnefoy talks of signifieds as having become 'unreal' in their contemporary or 'modernist' casting. Bonnefoy briefly evokes another of his past colleagues at the Collège, this time Michel Foucault with his working analytical and historical notion of an 'archaeology' of knowledge. To take on such a notion, Bonnefoy suggests, has the effect of complicating irredeemably our access to concepts which come at us from the past and now resolutely assert their mobility and their otherness. It is important to see the point clearly, here. Bonnefoy's anxiety about the way signifieds seem to have become 'unreal' is not a participation in a simplistic view of what is sometimes called the 'free play of signifiers', said by many contemporary critics to form the distinctiveness of what literature aspires to put on display. From within the shadow still cast by criticism of a structuralist kind, certainly in Britain, readers might almost think they were being asked to believe that practitioners of language were able to achieve the impossible – a complete emancipation of word from the structures of possible sense. Moreover, there is another, still limited view of what is involved in structuralist readings and their aftermath. This view suggests that such approaches allow for a self-contained, complacent world of 'text', to which all endeavour is reduced and which can assert its own values, its own modes of interpreting and reading, perhaps even its own ideology.

But such are not the conceptions of 'text' which Bonnefoy seeks to engage with, nor the ones he seeks to challenge and develop. His aim, once again, is to focus on that power which poetry might have to grapple with essential qualities of existing, of relating and speaking. The Barthesian 'text' that seems to fascinate Bonnefoy is not one that can be circumscribed simply because it attempts to come to terms with the ways in which convention allows expression by limiting it. Barthes continually suggests that it is only by virtue of rhetorically manufacturing a rationalist detachment that the effects of convention *can* be circumscribed. It is for this reason that Bonnefoy evokes Barthes's notion of text in terms of shadows as well as galaxies and constellations. Indeed he seems to be echoing Barthes's own metaphoric presentation of the idea of text in *S/Z*,

The Pleasure of the Text, and elsewhere. Barthes's notion of the 'plural' text soliciting different but related readings can turn out to be as alienating as it is liberating, since it carries with it signals that purchase on what we do when we speak or read or write is eluding us.

But these 'shadows' obscuring our knowledge of what we do as we act linguistically need not require a passive, resigned alienation from us. In characterising contemporary approaches to the signified as 'unreal', Bonnefoy seems elliptically to be engaging with Jean-Paul Sartre's way of accounting for human consciousness in terms of freedom. The French word here is *irréel* – not only 'unreal', but perhaps even more: 'without contact with reality'. This is the quality Sartre assigns to constructions of objects, as well as situations, in the imagination. In *L'Imaginaire*, on which Sartre worked just before and during the Second World War, these constructions are 'without contact with reality' since they are not produced in interaction with new data, or with the ever-changing constructions of experience that go on in perception. For Sartre, perception and imagination are two modes of consciousness continually in tension with one another; the one designating, organising, shaping, using; the other synthesising, totalising, capturing. But the effects and the prizes of imaginary totalising are ambivalent, for it is based on what we already know of what we try to imagine. Nothing new can be added to such constructions, they lie *outside*, somewhere other than in the continual conventional, ideological interplay of self and others. And yet this static, global account of a state of knowledge, and of a subjective situation, acquires power – exactly because of its own negative characteristics. The networks of meaning – sense and significance – are accounted for here and mastered in a kind of momentary eternity.

Like Sartre, Bonnefoy turns to the image again in trying to say the power of poetry – or is this a mirage?

> I will call image that impression of a finally, fully incarnated reality that comes to us, paradoxically, from words turned away from the incarnation. Images, world-images, in the sense, I think, that Baudelaire understood it when he wrote, at one of the most tormented moments of his poetic intuition: 'the cult of images, my great, my only, my primitive passion'. Images, marks of that extravagant brightness [*éclat*] lacking in the liquid greyness of our days, but which language allows us when it is moulded to that constant thirst we call dream, and when it is kneaded by that dream like a maternal breast.

A Christian-inspired aspiration to fulfilment suggested by the notion of 'incarnation' is in many ways at odds with the embattled Sartrean notion of freedom. Sartre's freedom is one to which we are condemned: we are submitted to a logic of consciousness ('*pour-soi*') forcing forever renewed realisations of a freedom imposed and imposing, and of a world used. Used but not mastered. For this is a world continuously disestablished and reconstituted in terms of new situations, within which assertion and affirmation are a matter of failed but unstoppable struggles for domination. Sartre would seem to be abandoning the metaphysical revelation of essential truths Bonnefoy hopes to find in the poetic involvement with words. 'Existence precedes essence' is one of Sartre's fundamental and most notorious conclusions and working principles. But at the same time, Sartre *is* dealing in essential properties – those of consciousness: the elements of its functioning, the attempts to account for itself (and even perhaps to assert its own beginning) that propel it. Perception, linked up to prose in Sartre's world, inevitably drifts into the imaginary mode of consciousness and into the poetic. Assertive linguistic acts and acts of perception trigger the wild dream of fixing their own purpose, of drawing a path to the terms by which they exist. And these are the very dreams and paths which make up the networks of the Image, and provide its deathly stillness – what Bonnefoy calls its 'melancholic genius' – with the attributes of revelation and creativity. Bonnefoy pays homage, here, to the lure and the magnificence of this 'dream' by evoking it in terms of the maternal, of incarnation, of an original body.

Douve

On the Movement and the Immobility of Douve (1953) is Bonnefoy's first full-scale book of poetry. Its title signals a problematic fascination with sequence and with naming. Movement seems valued only in so far as it engenders the motionless and thus denies itself; at the same time, the motionless is feared for the complacency and the asphyxia it suggests. Both face each other off in a play of double negatives in which there is no winner, no 'either/or', no 'both'. Where might such a play run, and what would be its name? Douve is not a proper name, as the capital letter suggests it should be. But it is a noun meaning a moat. The strangeness of using a noun as a name seems to invite us to wonder more acutely about the features of the moat designated by the noun. Is it a defence, or just a space between two areas? Is battle joined or suspended? What part is played in this ambivalence by the female, alluded to by the symbolism of the water in the moat? John Naughton suggests that the most evocative way of reading this ambivalence is to think of 'Douve' as a kind of French '*dovè?*', Italian for 'where?'.

At the same time, we *can* place this space with no name, it is known to us as death. Douve has died and the poetic voice in the book addresses himself to this event from the position of lover.

What are the ways in which the event of death exerts its fascination, and what are the ways in which this can be told? The first sequence of poems in *Douve* is entitled *Theatre*. What Bonnefoy is working with here is not purely the idea of a secure allocation of different roles and positions allowing us to speak. It is more an investigation of our *sense* of this allocation. It is a grappling with the temporality and the mobility of an awareness that we *do* occupy positions as we speak. It is an investigation of the acts themselves of speaking and addressing, the experiences and the aspirations that such acts trigger. I want to discuss two examples from this sequence of poems in the book – *Theatre* II and *Theatre* III.

Existing is imperfect, the sensual intoxication of it unrevealing. At some moment in the past, at some other moment in the timelessness in which intimacy seems cast, Douve appears now, at any new moment of reading or remembering, to send out images of what is lacking. But this imagery is not a capturing. The moment of speaking is unspecifiable – 'you would say'. And the rhetoric is one of correction, although the imperfection evoked is as lacking in definition as the moment in which it is imagined – '"*rather* ivy, the way it clings..."'

The effects of this 'rather' extend throughout this small poem. The final, uncompleted statement is affirmative, while denying this affirmativeness a ground to stand on: 'rather this wind...' than what? The previous bit of this broken speech uses 'rather...' in a further syntactical construction that confirms the contemplative way in which particles of experience are being related to each other. '"Rather in the mountains this village to die in"' – are we in opposition or in juxtaposition to the cutting edge of the sun's probing (an abrasive reappraisal, perhaps, of the Homer's famous 'rosy-fingered dawn')? But in either case, there is a violence which is pursued, the appeal of violence is explored. It is a violence directed against conclusion, against the developments that the narrative artefacts of language seem to prescribe.

In inaugurating this 'no' beyond negation, a 'no' directed at any form of affirming or pointing, against any hope of living comfortably with language, Bonnefoy turns to the image of the stone, as he will do frequently throughout his work: '"Rather ivy, the way it clings to the stones of its night..."' (I am also thinking of the many poems entitled 'Une Pierre'/'A Stone' in *Pierre écrite/ Written Stone* [1965]). But can we call this an 'image'? At least in terms of their content, this phrase and those around it seek to circumvent the play of associations that might conventionally make up an 'image' and allow us to interpret it. In this continually once-removed syntactic space of the 'rather...', the ivy is attached to stones in its own night, without reference to others, without 'exits' or 'roots' that it might share with other experiences and precedents. It is in the spectre of such a deathly, inhuman non-sharing that Bonnefoy discovers the quality of presence.

In terms of the deconstructive approach to metaphysics set in motion by Derrida, or of the textual ethics imagined by Roland Barthes, or again of the unbuilding of egoist delusion pursued in Lacanian psychoanalysis, nothing would seem to place Bonnefoy further outside the bounds or the obligations of contemporary French thought than such an apprehension of presence. And yet the paths that lead Bonnefoy into this affirmation of a human subject holding its own against the tramlines of speech seem to embrace those imagined by Roland Barthes in his own youthful attempts to fabricate a 'writing degree zero'. For both Barthes and Bonnefoy, writing aspires to be 'exempted from the obligations of sense', as Barthes puts it. And yet for both, writing is itself propelled by a fascinated awareness that such exemption is the stuff of dreams.

But such dreams, Bonnefoy suggests here, can be enacted, transformed into gestures watched and exchanged. In a violent wind of torn cries and garments, the 'graph lining' of our mentality into packages of response is metaphorically swept aside leaving memory blank and open. The unknown and the novel cohabit with the blank, they depend on it, just as presence here, after all, seems to depend on absence: 'and you reigned at last absent from my brain'. Here, seemingly, is a moment of achievement, where an interlocutor dominates by vacating the space she occupies, leaving the other speaker's own space equally empty but nevertheless *there*. In these two small poems, a theatre of interplay has unfolded between establishing and disestablishing, solidifying and melting, between making sense and refusing to, between speech and burial. And on this stage, to the accompaniment of some sort of pre-cultural, other-cultural drums reminiscent of Rimbaud, the male speaker is offered an imaginary grasping of his own moulding, the moulding of his mentality and of his body.

But this is still only near the beginning of *Douve*. It would be disappointing to pre-empt what Bonnefoy seems to be working for here, or to attribute too soon to his writing a realisation of Rimbaud's impassioned, urgent and continually renewed aspiration to *'posséder la vérité dans une âme et un corps'* – 'to take possession of truth within the forms of a single soul and a single body'. Indeed, there is a dynamic tentativeness in Bonnefoy's simultaneously poetic and metaphysical pursuit of a blank presence beyond category and even beyond word. This is expressed at one of the most basic levels on which *Douve* functions. I am thinking of the interplay in the *Theatre* section in particular between the prose poem and the versified one.

Douve, as an open book, continually places prose and verse simultaneously under the reader's gaze. This gives the effect of a continual hesitation emanating from the book at one of its most immediate points of contact with the reader. Of course, our sense of the 'poetic' is not limited to language, or to language that is versified or rhymed, or again to language that is emphatically rhythmed. Perhaps we allow a poetic response to any kind of expression that seems to display a sense of wonder at its own effects, and at the way these effects seem to proliferate the more we turn our attention to them.

Many French poets from the nineteenth century onwards engage in an unsteady, balletic sounding-out of the differing implications of versified and prose poetry. Baudelaire wrote versions of some of his most famous texts in each mode – a practice which has continued to fascinate and perplex his readers. Without suggesting that the prose-poem is in any way more prosaic than the one in verse, Baudelaire's work in the medium suggests, typically, a further challenge to the aspirations of verse, as though poems in verse and in prose were each built on suspicion of the seductive pull of poetic achievement at large. As I have suggested, the Baudelairean fascination with the image acts as a trigger to Bonnefoy's own interrogation of poetry and of what it sets out to achieve. Baudelaire's suspicious approach to his own enterprise as a poet takes on the qualities of a metaphysical terror in his prose poems, many of which act as a kind of confession: 'must we eternally suffer, or else eternally take flight from beauty?...Stop prodding my desire and tempting my vanity! The study of beauty is a duel in which the artist cries out in terror before defeat' ('The *Confiteor* of the Artist', from Baudelaire's *Paris Spleen*). The Baudelairean study of beauty-in-prose involves a sustained, escape-proof encounter with artifice and with hubris, in which Baudelaire lays bare a grotesque, mountebank-style complacency that continually threatens to accompany the sensations and the images of poetic success. This arrogance and delusion are triggered by an involvement with poetry itself. Baudelaire wryly enacts this ironic turn of events by exclaiming at the conclusion of 'À une heure du matin'/'At One O'Clock in the Morning': 'Dear Lord God! grant me the grace of producing a few beautiful verses that would prove to me that I'm not the least of men, that I'm not inferior to those I despise.'

Rimbaud, a later seeker of poetic perfection through artifice – of a poetic *tabula rasa* – similarly finds the attempt to undo poetic hubris and complacency to be an element of a 'Season in Hell'. Once again, the forms of this hell are those of prose, the casting of the poetic enterprise is ironic and perverse. Perhaps Bonnefoy, in response, seeks a poetry free both of complacency and perversity? His ultimate turning away from the brutal building by negation of Rimbaud, as well as from the violence of Surrealism, would seem to suggest this. But in *Douve*, the violence of death is in play. And yet the hesitation between prose and verse in the *Theatre* chapter of *Douve* signals not so much a poetry proceeding by its own dismemberment, but more a tentative inching towards inaugurating and naming. But this is still an inching that proceeds by interrogation; verse and prose seem constantly to be turning the tables on one another.

Compare with each other two facings-off in the series: *Theatre* X and XI, and *Theatre* XII and XIII. Though succeeding each other, the relations within each pair of embracing to losing, of the positioned to the indefinite, the structured to the blank, are not constant. Each such pole in these dialogues seems as attractive as the other, and each seems promoted in verse as well as prose. In *Theatre* X, the carnal presence of Douve as corpse provokes measureless sensuousness – a presence 'heard rustling' in a space with no dimension. The black-princes and Douve herself act as myths that combat and combine. The activities of devouring and ridding are transformed into the creation of a web-like edifice, and now a spider appears with multiple mythological attributes. For Ariadne, lover of Theseus, and for Penelope, wife of Odysseus, strings and weaving represent both guile and conviction. For Medea, spurned lover of Jason to whom she has contrived to give the Golden Fleece, an enchanted web is an instrument for destroying her rival by fire. But these associations, though immanent, are muffled here rather than displayed. The spider contrives to 'illuminate', to grasp, to recast this web of meanings as a vision, rather than as something which might ring or bind or field.

In *Theatre* XI, the other poem in the pair, the quality in verse generally which seems to advertise its own power to organise and to impose form seems equally to work against itself and to fail to deliver. A single verse form is in fact not sustained in this short poem, since the lines are either in the Classical, twelve-syllable alexandrine, or they use metres with fewer syllables, and the overall effect of this oscillation is not so much one of "freedom" as tentativeness, or even vulnerability. Moreover, the labyrinthine networks of sensation ('covered by...silent humus'), of precedent ('the world', 'the life and death of sand') and of eroticised intellectual aspiration ('secret knowledge', 'teeth bared as if for love') all serve to articulate the demise of Douve's lover even in his own process of visualising Douve's corpse. Certainly, once again this is a death that in one sense seems actively to be desired – a kind of unthinkable cutting of the Gordian knots binding expression to emulation, a cutting which seems to happen in *bodily* as well as cultural terms. But here, the very intensity of such desire seems to make it fluid, without adequate vessel, and hence 'unbearable'; neither contained nor sustained in the forms and metaphors of the poem. Perhaps this is its salvation.

But in the next pair – *Theatre* XII and *Theatre* XIII – the situation, in some sense at least, seems to be reversed. Prose initially appears to promote the uncaptured, verse the sustained. The ordering pretensions of verse seem momentarily to have been restored. The prose image of Douve as corpse is one of a space invaded, embattled branches cast shadows that line her face, tree-roots mine her flesh; a startling urban chaos casts its echoes and remnants of its imagery over her. In verse, on the other hand, the images used to evoke Douve's features are those of light, of three-dimensional ease and power ('turning eagles'), and these are features which the narrator-lover is able to 'hold...cold'. And yet at this very moment, the metre seems to drift over into a 'free' verse stretching the limits of metre. To 'hold...cold' seems to be a gesture that is loving and valued exactly in so far as the captivating power of imagery loses its grip. In the previous line, the penultimate one of the short poem, the emphasising of the 'turning eagles' as 'image' truncates the line and brings the poem to an abrupt halt. The narrator holds down his lover without holding her, constructs her only to the extent of losing his power to build in metaphor, verse and image; he imagines her in a realm – 'at a depth' – where imagination loses direction. Verse regenerates in the slipstream of its own collapse. In the same way, at the conclusion of the *prose* poem, the other poem which makes up the pair, we find a love imagined beyond death. Here is Douve once again, exultant and participating in the 'knotted' light of the 'plateaux', not a light that simply illuminates, but one that seems to mould itself to the acerbic thorniness of cultural as well as sensual matter, beyond which, or even *in* which Douve seems able to come up for air. Prose and verse meet where both see through the glass darkly.

The 'theatre' of this opening section of *Douve* is a poetic meditation – in which a sense of the poetic is at once the object and the means of examination – on some of the basic features of making statements and making sense: speaker, word, listener. What does it mean to name? What does listening to a name and coming to terms with it involve us in? A later section of *Douve* is entitled *Sole Witness* – witnessing perhaps the weight of an audience and an interrogation of it. Equally, this is a celebration of a desire to delve into, to probe and to pass beyond the force of this ever-present and appropriative audience.

A Christian dimension to this poetic sinking into meaning itself, and the ways it made, is immanent here. In the Bible, the only true witnesses are the witnesses to the Resurrection. In Christian dogma, moreover, the garb of the priest bears witness to the priest's faith. And yet at the same time, within Christian belief, the Sole True Witness to God is Jesus Christ. Human beings, in this sense, cannot be 'true witnesses' to their own belief, nor find a 'true' language to express it. The same tension between Truth made tangible, and the disintegration of Truth, is apparent in Christian thinking on the *logos*. The Word has the power to make God present. But this is not a singular power. It is seated in the Gospels – which themselves cast nets into the Old Testament. In this sense, the Christian Word is both prospective and archaeological. And archaeology, though evoking edifices and structures, also deals in labyrinths and ruins. Once again, where is there place for the speaking, or believing, 'I'?

The fifth poem in this sequence of six called *Sole Witness* takes the form of a sustained question – where the inauguration, where the event in Douve's deathly state? But in the first stanza at least, the interrogative form is effaced rather than sustained, ending as it does with a full-stop rather than the question-mark that seems anticipated by the syntax. So that the associations of despair triggered by the lyrical opening gambit 'Where now...' seem momentarily to be countered by the definitive statement of novelty and inventiveness in the final line of the stanza – though, once again, this is a paradoxical inventiveness, a capacity to create silence. But this is an announcement of inventiveness that seems enveloped in positive omens. The stag carries us into medieval iconographic scripts. Here images of stags, representing Christ, are a kind of living proof that the unknowable *can* be represented. A different, un-fixed, continually self-differentiating interplay of the natural and the cultural is momentarily established. It heralds a path to an essential justice based on the values of *ex*pression, it declares a violent open-ness, a generalised *ex*pulsion into a wordless, bodily *word* that by its very impregnability is instantaneously past – *'fut ouverte'*.

And so the reign of question and of doubt has returned, the great spectre of 'Where...?' has resumed its engulfing flight at the end of the poem. Where the just violence of invention, the gift renewed of word and body? The stag no longer seems to roam independently within its own re-configuration of the interaction of nature and culture.

Instead, it is chased to frontiers. It is now a feature of Douve's dress, a part of the public face of the event that is the death of Douve. An other degree of awareness is introduced of ways in which gestures are received, shanghaied within indefinite cultural networks and tendrils that do, after all, make images perform. However surrealistically, anarchistically, ludically inappropriate the comparisons may seem of Douve's dress to a lake of sand, to the cold, to the stag hounded at frontiers, here they serve to activate that sense of the way associations are recognised and placed. Sand inescapably evokes time, here provisionally contained in the circumference of a lake, by contrast to the flowing waters of a river. Douve has indeed 'returned' – to a place in the networks of metaphoric sense and purpose. What is the beauty of this return?

A sacred, acrid, asphyxiated and violently *open* sense of naming is the gift that seems to be proffered. Titles in the rest of *Douve* include the words 'True Name', 'True Body', along with the repeated returns of 'A Voice'. This sketches a kind of testimony to an imagined birth of a new interlacing of sensuality and sense. The visceral force of naming now seems to hold its own against the public impact of the name itself. But the title 'True Name' is an anxious one. It is a further allusion to Christian meditation: the only true name is impossible, indeed prohibited – it is the name of God. The beginning of sense-making can not be named, just as the violent new beginning incarnated in 'Douve' is itself *not* a name...

And yet in 'True Name', in the emphatic 'I will name' that opens the first and last stanzas of the poem, the narrating 'I' seems momentarily to take charge not only of the name, but also of that public impact of the name. This future tense of 'I will name' is more than a deluded expression of power over public reaction to words from now until the end of time. It is an expression of a further *sense* of time, of an imaginary capacity to attribute horizons to it, however mobile, and to explore them. Bonnefoy's embattled 'I' in these lines is still the embattled lover of death, the lover who aspires to the generosity with which to embrace the degree zero of a deathly beginning. This present enunciation here of a future naming carries with it a violence which both signals and inaugurates the will to think time beyond the conventions of history, to espouse dialogue beyond the conventions that allow sense and its exchange.

But this 'beyond' is not a Gnostic assertion of a spirituality irreconcilable with the body. The violence of 'True Name' bears witness also to the condition of existence-in-convention, just as much as to the enforced contours of the body, and to the shapes that mould our sense of the body. But now that violence of condition, and the violence of the desire to resist it, form an imaginary whole, an imaginary body. Within this body naming and silence, holding and losing, desiring and destroying combine but also refuse to. Douve both is and is not in dialogue with her lover, she both exists and fails to exist outside the lines of the narrating, imagining 'I'. This space of merciless aggression but also of freedom, of stability and transience, of memory loved and lost, this space to which no paths lead, or only dark ones which cannot be called 'mine' or 'ours' but only 'yours'; this space where 'I' dominates, but is then dissolved and returned as 'you'; this space is a name, a body, a *place*.

Place

What has been called a metaphysics of place is a predominant concern of Bonnefoy's. Throughout his poetry a sense of place is striven for in recurrent motifs evoking the concrete and the familiar: stones passed from hand to hand; a breast or a shoulder revealed and touched; an almond tree and the paths of a much-loved garden; boats crossing from one shore to the other. In each of these recurrent clusters of association, Bonnefoy searches out paths from the present to the past, from the particular to the indefinite, the enclosed to the embracing. In this way, Bonnefoy seeks to re-affirm a sense of poetic purpose, a confidence in the power to name and to conceive beyond the networks of convention, and to re-discover in these networks the imprints of a spiritual dimension.

> Is it not with the void that the word is engaged in an ancient battle? It is possible that an act of establishing presence – that lost light testified to by Baudelaire's poetics – is also the origin of the word. And for my own part, I am ready, within a general process of poetry's becoming, within the word as invention or as return, and so as to walk on that path that will reveal itself to be the only true path, I am ready to affirm extravagantly a *here and now* which is already, I admit, an over there and a long ago, which no longer exists, which has been stolen from us, but which eternally – in its finite temporality – and universally – in its spacial infirmity – is the only conceivable place, the only place worthy of the name of place. In modern French poetry there is a procession of the Grail, made up of the most vital objects on this earth – a tree, a face, a stone – and it is those that we must name. Everything we hope for is at stake.

In this passage from *L'Acte et le lieu de la poésie/ The Act and the Place of Poetry*, from the book of essays entitled *L'Improbable/ The Improbable*, Bonnefoy longs for names re-named, names re-placed, for a word saved and speakers healed. Again, he returns to his speculation on Baudelaire – who for Bonnefoy is quintessentially the poet of the here and now and of the immediate. But for Bonnefoy, Baudelaire's seems a crippled, distressed sense of the moment – veering to a sense of exile, of capture and defeat. Bonnefoy allusively homes in on Baudelaire's sustained and yet paradoxical evocation of the tangible, of the sensual and the material. A passing scent, a passer-by, a decrepit performer – such are the triggers of Baudelaire's poetic reverie, the elements of the integration he imagines of the psychic and the physical, an integration that would go beyond mere immobility and formula. But for Bonnefoy, Baudelaire's hold on the tangible paradoxically gives rise to a kind of obsession with the fragment, a psychic adherence to the fragmentary. This makes his pursuit of a dynamic concentration of everything eclectic and disparate seem like the stuff of pure artifice. In this essay, Bonnefoy's response to this lure of the fragment takes the form of an impassioned speculation about the energy needed to *begin*, to make a beginning – an energy displayed no more disinterestedly than by Baudelaire himself. This beginning involves re-inventing the notion of endings, of death and of loss.

And for Bonnefoy, to re-invent, in this sense, is not to repeat. It does not trigger the embattled Sartrean '*témoignage*', the bearing witness to existential, unchangeable properties of our condition and of our interaction with others. Bonnefoy strives to take us beyond continual presentations and re-presentations of essentialist conflict – conflict with mortality, with the appropriativeness of others. But Bonnefoy himself avoids dismissing the intellectual grit of other thinkers. The Sartrean notion of position seems allusively embraced in Bonnefoy's vision of place, along with the Sartrean sensation of our positioning *accounted for* in an image – the image of a name. For Bonnefoy in this essay, Dante's 'Beatrice!' inaugurates again a fundamental poetic desire to *'se défaire du monde'* ('to untie oneself from the world'), to be unbound from the agents of our dispossession – time, space, matter. These signals of mortality are dissipated in the pleasure of naming, as though a name encompassed the sensual depth of what we named and allowed us to revel in it momentarily. The repetition of such moments of dissipation and imagined power is the stuff of knowledge, Bonnefoy suggests. And what an ambivalent prize it is: knowledge, that agg-ressive nostalgia which packages and seals our dispossession in the form of absolutes – manageable, comfortable, unchanging.

So this is the death with which Bonnefoy would have no truck; his efforts to reinvent death involve its metamorphosis. In *The Act and the Place of Poetry*, Bonnefoy takes issue with a certain kind of speculation which he sees as evolving from Mallarmé's writing – a speculation which, for Bonnefoy at least, seems to equate the concept of absence with that of creativity. The unbuilding of the subservience of signifier to signified, rather than consistently allowing a sustained, fascinated investigation of sense itself, its sensations and its irregularity, triggers Bonnefoy's seemingly most heartfelt fear – the fear of abstraction. Once again, abstraction in Bonnefoy's thinking signals the seductiveness of pure form, molecular marks of sense, units in a structural purpose deprived of visceral foundation. And for Bonnefoy, the content that would return to such hubristic formal constructions their life-blood is built from the subjective. The place where the meaning of the pronoun 'I' might be unearthed, and where an elemental sense of existence, of objects and of others might be apprehended, is the body.

This sense of a 'subjective blood beating in event and object' is embraced by Bonnefoy in a sustained resistance to the voracity of the ego, and of the rationalist ego in particular. But this resistance is not a turning to the body as erotically self-regarding. As Bonnefoy grasps it, the body is itself situated temporally and spatially, opened out to the obscurity of its own becoming. As we stand in a temple, the manipulation of proportion makes us dream, perhaps,

30

of an existence free of the indefinite, of the incomplete and the circumstantial. But we also celebrate the unpredictable, an unexpected present-ness in the sight of an alter or the smell of a crypt. For Bonnefoy, shadow falling through a window on the carved face of a statue signals a shattering of symmetry, a well opening out down into 'the unknowable depths of place', giving sense and sensation to our beginnings and endings. For Bonnefoy, this celebration of the obscure is what binds the experience of place to the practice of literature.

This is an obscurity of aura and quality, rather than of concept or system. By way of a challenge to the reader, Bonnefoy in this essay signals his commitment to this form of obscurity by invoking readings of Racine – superficially that most desperate of writers faced with the collapse of reason. Racinian figures live by impassioned images of dominance over object and requirement. But in this very detachment and the obsession with it, Bonnefoy perceives a Socratic sort of simplicity in approaches to death and in the acceptance of it. The Classical armour of heroic, courtly figurations of the self not so much gives way to, but actually allows a melting of signs, of the man-made and the artificial in the heat of a kind of present indefinite. But is this smelting actually to be seen and experienced – other than in the mobility, the controlled improvisation manufactured in Bonnefoy's approach to the essay form itself?

Bonnefoy wonders. He wonders about the compulsive appeal of incest, frightening for Bonnefoy in its perversity, ingrained in the body of Phèdre. Might this "perversity" not prove to be a basic form of that bodily interaction with others that it is the mission of Bonnefoy's poetry to uncover and to liberate? And on the other hand, he wonders about the Classical figure of the misanthrope, locked in the arid application of a set of ideals itself restricted to precedent. Perhaps the Racinian venture is, after all, flawed. Where can we find that forging together, so urgently pursued by Bonnefoy, of a love of place, and the heretical, Gnostic pursuit of a pure spirituality? In the here and now of this moment in Bonnefoy's essay, at this crossroads in his effort to combine integrated experience with an unpredictable one, his prize is what he calls 'the vacant ego' of French Classical poetry. Its marks are the suspended animation of formalised seventeenth-century orangeries which Bonnefoy imagines empty – both in this essay and in *Douve*; or the Racinian vision of a thousand paths leading off from the voice of the supremacist's delusion and dissolving it. Here is a poetry waiting indefinitely for an intuitive gesture to make it whole.

In *Douve*, such gestures are made up of assertion and its undermining, tentativeness and its affirmation. The title of the last section of the book – 'True Place' – seems to herald that this dynamic may finally have been resolved. In Christian experience, the True Place is the Cross. But the Cross is not the place of God. Where, then, is the 'True Place' in Bonnefoy's book?

One poem that makes up this 'Place' is the 'Lieu de la Salamandre'/'Place of the Salamander'. The salamander is a creature which, it was once thought, could crawl through fire unharmed. Here it is admired for bearing witness to its own elemental existence, for surviving emblematically as an elemental being. The narrator expresses a sense of his own fulfilment at the accord, the involvement of this wholly bodily being with the 'stars', which here suggest not so much the universal, as the extensive, the indefinitely tactile qualities of matter itself. And yet any resolution here takes the form of dialogue. The salamander is an 'accomplice', a friendly 'allegory', a rhetorical construction, but also a *presence* in the poem. But nevertheless, this elemental presence is made up of the cultural and the social. Perhaps this unresolved tension in the poem is its salvation, the *place* of its own crossing, through fire, of the material and the spiritual. For the flames are themselves metaphoric, this poem and the book as it draws to a close both express an awareness of this and a joy in it. The salamander is an animal, as such out of the scope of the lines we read and that Bonnefoy has composed. Sharing in the salamander's accord with the elemental is as much a matter of feint as is the salamander's own sudden immobility caught in the gaze of the human. And yet from such imaginary, impossible foreclosing of cultural contracts, Bonnefoy evokes a new mythology, 'the purest myth', a language of aspiration that we could at least *imagine*, almost, to be beyond the metaphoric and the artificial. This myth made flesh derives, once again, from violence, from silence, from fire, but also, here, from a community comprising narrator, reader, and the figure of a *living* companion. Suddenly, an unrepeatable and yet highly familiar moment – sunbaked wall, motionless salamander, two people engrossed – at once leaps from the page and is restricted to it, defying simple pigeonholing. Here is a community imagined at its most fundamental level, emphasising its human proportion, drawing the social into the intimate. Perhaps the 'accomplice' is, then, also the narrator's companion. The two stand at the window, accomplices in a subjective spanning of language and silence, the inert and the fulfilled.

How far, then, the idea and the sensations of place have allowed

the book to develop. It began by presenting the only hope of fulfil-
ment in terms of a violent *tabula rasa* and of death. How different
the quality of truth in 'True Body', the penultimate poem in the
Last Acts chapter, from that of 'Place of the Salamander'. As I have
tried to emphasise, the sense of place *is* bodily for Bonnefoy. And
yet at this earlier stage in the book, the desire for a body and a
language made one, for a pure Word, still takes a desperate form.
The narrator revels in Douve's deathly silence *by silencing her again*
– through his own acts and his own writer's will. I am thinking of
the assertions – made *in* the poem and for which it is responsible –
of 'silenced that voice' and 'walled in those eyes'. The marriage of
word and the depths of the body is ultimately only 'accomplished'
here as the narrator wilfully affirms that his own acts of naming and
knowing are located in this nether region beyond the man-made,
and that they are to be understood in terms of it. Not that the poem
is any less dramatic or urgent in its tone for that. Read in this way,
it remains an urgent plea, accomplished on the imaginary and rhet-
orical levels and there alone, for a subjective beginning in speaking
and naming.

In the next chapter, where the narrator imagines 'Douve speak-
ing', the capacity to begin still seems conquered by embracing viol-
ence – now the violence of a purification by fire of which Phoenix
is the embodiment, and which is a motif running through the book.
I am thinking of the second poem in this chapter entitled 'A Voice'
(page 108). Pride is taken in a scorched earth, in charred roads
leading back to a re-building of 'the pride we once knew' – perhaps
an unyielding 'force' allowing these imagined protagonists to keep
intact the wild dream of autonomy.

But there is another dimension to this poem. There is a liber-
ating, alternative way in which, simultaneously, it can be read. The
'Voice' is not only that of the narrator, but of Douve, that being, we
imagine, that exists somewhere entirely other, and which is given
voice by the artifice of the writing here. Now the poem appears
built to open out to a kingdom valuable because it is 'undone', to
the 'ashes' of cultivation and of property, and to the devastation of
a body stuck in orthodox relations to others. This other 'I' in the
poem stretching herself on this ravaged body, and sounding alarm
bells in the subjective worlds of the reader, is quite explicitly *invented*
by Bonnefoy. It is an attempt to build a poem on a basis that the
poem itself would gloriously fail to contain. It is an attempt to turn
the self-avowing rhetoric of the poem against itself and to begin
again. But where is the way out?

In 'Place of the Salamander', beginning is suggested in Bonnefoy's evocation of a spontaneous sense of community. The figures in the poem, with the readers *of* the poem, watch the motionless salamander, and on this basis, we sense the possibility of a new mythology – the 'pure myth' – through which to represent our sense of being alive. But the salamander is itself imbued with mythological significance – its resistance to fire, etc – which is already in place as we speak, and which we cannot do away with. Just as we are here reading poems, which already have a range of ideological features to them which differentiate them from other kinds of language. There is a mysterious 'secret demon' in the previous poem, a demon that is 'never buried' and that is there to be fought on the threshold of the new and 'arduous dawn'. Perhaps it is that demon which makes us dream wildly of stepping beyond our place in language, and which endlessly bemoans its own failure.

Denouncing the Image, loving images

The rhetoric of *Douve* is characterised by a dynamic of completion and fragmentation which involves the image and the body. This dynamic is complicated by the fact that each of its poles – completion, fragmentation – is presented as both desirable and suspect. But suspect as the poetic image is, oppressive and foreclosing as an imaginary encompassing of mortality might be, these are the practical and intellectual mainstays of Bonnefoy's poetic examination of our inwardness and of our subjectivity. In *Presence and Image*, Bonnefoy describes his ambivalent objective as 'to denounce the Image, all the better to love images'.

I have suggested that what Bonnefoy's thinking and terminology share with Roland Barthes's is a dissatisfaction with the essentially conventional nature of the sign – both as an intellectual obsession and as an existential feature of any speaker's condition. For Barthes, though, the herding of our mentality into conventional moulds of response and of desire involves all the networks of ideology. Knowledge is an ideological construct, Barthes reminds us. But particularly in his later works, from his self-styled autobiography *Roland Barthes* onwards, he adds a further element to his thinking. (Perhaps *Douve* is also a self-styled autobiography, in that it is a book which seeks to delve into the ways we attempt to think of ourselves as constructed, whole beings.) Barthes suggests that attempts to undo the effects of ideology, of a thinking that proceeds by vested interest and that incessantly reduces the many to the one, tend themselves to engender an involvement with these same ideological effects. A competitive vying for methodological supremacy – along the lines of 'who will be more progressive than whom?' – ensues among professional critics and thinkers. This *replicates* the assertions of authority – both ideological and personal – which in many ways it is the purpose of both Barthes's and Bonnefoy's writing to undermine.

Barthes's response to this, like Bonnefoy's, is aesthetic. No critical theory, no science of signs can untie sensation from signification, or desire from its permissible forms. But nor can any literary practice, either, however ludic or violent. But what it can do is seek to return to images thrown up in life their temporality and their inwardness. Barthes attempts this in developing a rhetoric of the fragment in his later books, particularly in *Fragments d'un discours amoureux / Fragments of a Lover's Discourse* and the book on photography called *La Chambre claire / Camera Lucida*. Each of these fragments acts in the books as a resistance to the establishing of discursive or methodological authority. This is perhaps particulary striking in the case of *Fragments of a Lover's Discourse* – a book on love by a one-time 'structuralist' thinker. This book is admired, albeit rather grudgingly, for the quality of its writing by Marguerite Duras, the contemporary novelist of the erotic and a writer who is otherwise resolutely opposed to critics and intellectuals. Barthes's linking of the experiences of love with the notion of a discourse is not an attempt to systematise the erotic and the intimate. Barthes's book of fragments or bits is a courageous attempt to express the ways in which, as lovers, we imagine words and sensations uniquely ours, or rather structured as a discourse that moulds itself seamlessly to our own desires. Each bit of writing is devoted to a particular joy, a particular way in which intimate desire is matched by the precedents which make it orthodox and acceptable and *known* – hotels, bars, gossip, jealousy...By the same token, each fragment also draws attention to this ingrained intertwining of the orthodox and the erotic and in this way seeks to resist it, to call it to a halt.

And yet the manufacturing of such open-ended bittiness, this resistance to the glutinous quality of the way our desires seem magnetically attracted to the familiar and the permissible, is purely artificial. It belongs on the level of rhetorical expertise. It belongs to that same domain of pleasurable mastery of verbal and amorous discourse which the fragment itself seeks to disrupt. So much is even advertised, ironically, by classifying the fragments in neat, alphabetical order at the back of the book. Barthes's own textuality thus serves to manufacture repeated gaps and intervals, repeated pauses for breath in that desperate and false hope of exploiting models to capture others and our desire for them. But this same writer's detachment also triggers once again the process of imaginary capturing. It encourages the illusion that by writing and reading, we could free ourselves of the compulsion to conform and take control of this. The notion of text, as it develops in Barthes's work, bears witness to this indefinite, unpredictable mobility of the ways in which enclosed patterns of response, self-repeating models of thought, take desirable forms. Discourse, though rooted in ideology, though we experience it as given, in this way is seen to serve the narcissistic delusions, the self-enclosure on which we seem to rely so heavily in speaking and loving, and in inventing.

Barthes's writing bears witness to this paradoxical mobility of the ways in which ideological pressures take simultaneously desirable and oppressive forms. In this way, this is a writing which comes to grips, almost to blows, with that sense of textuality as alienating evoked by Bonnefoy in his inaugural lecture *Presence and Image*. As I suggested earlier, this sense of alienation derives from the possibility that we might only be able to make use of a signifying system, a system of making sense – make use of it rather than pass beyond it. In this way, the speaking subject would be radically deprived of a subjective sense of time, place and hope.

Both Barthes and Bonnefoy grieve for this loss. At the same time, both approach grief as a source of resistance to those narcissistic delusions of subjective wholeness and mastery which are encouraged, even generated by signifying systems of all kinds. As we know, the moat Bonnefoy seeks to erect in *Douve*, against the traps, against spontaneously produced mirages of fulfilment and vision, involves imagining a dead lover. This is a wilful, if itself imaginary, unbuilding of the sensual channels leading to and from the statements 'I love' and 'I possess'. Bonnefoy reconstructs Douve's bodily presence with themes of violence and a rhetoric of place. For Barthes, the dynamic involving grief, subjectivity, and imaginary or narcissistic delusion comes to a head in the photographic image.

This image can be perused pleasurably, calmly and in a well-behaved way, acting as a self-fulfilling prophecy to empirical habits of thinking or aesthetic habits of response. But the photographic image can also induce a kind of madness, for Barthes, a kind of ecstasy. Such a response would be prompted if what is an *image* of the real is allowed its absolutist quality, its imaginary, deluded power to mould itself to the indefinite *there-ness* of everything outside the speaker and outside the residually voyeuristic viewer. What returns in such moments to the viewer is a sense of love allowed in a terrifying setting aside of the ego. Such is the passage traversed by Barthes's *Camera Lucida*, his last full-blown book, as a response to the very real death of his mother. And such a confronting of grief, and a setting aside of the channels of signifying capture, is announced at the end of *Douve*. '*O notre force et notre gloire, pourrez-vous trouer la muraille des morts?*' In a poetics of the imaginary, the spectre of death, as well as its visceral violence, can be transformed into a regeneration of our desires. And at the level where such a poetry collapses, death is allowed to suggest a glorious, terrifying unwinding of the textures which bind us to desire itself.

Coda

And yet many readers may feel that Bonnefoy's essentialism – the fervour with which he insists that poetry should uncover the essential properties of existing – places him at odds with the resolutely slippery relativism of Barthes's thinking and writing. Barthes's own textual scatterings, his magnificent aspirations as a writer to allow for a scandalously 'untreatable' reality, might seem to unbuild the narcissistic pull more movingly, might seem both more grief-stricken and more democratic, than the confident, affirmative poetics of some of Bonnefoy's later books. Moreover, if such a chasm were to open out before us, in spite of all Bonnefoy's efforts to conceive of his own poetry and of the effects of contemporary French critical theory as interactive, then the implications of this could be very far-reaching. It would affect fundamentally the way we read different contemporary French poets, and our judgement of what we find there. A polarisation might develop in the demands made on us as readers by this poetry. On the one hand, we might be faced with affirmations of the power of the word, its power to reveal, to bring together, to transcend; on the other, with alienation, perversity, violence. On the one hand, with exhortations to consent to our condition as linguistic beings; on the other, with encouragement to resist the ideological effects of using language.

Such a polarisation of response can in itself be unhelpful, of course, in that it falsifies the complexity of the issues involved. Essentialism, for example, is a feature of a range of contemporary French thinkers' work whom we might also think of as having various bearings on the problem of ideology: a sociolinguistic essentialism in the case of Barthes, a bio-linguistic essentialism in the case of the psychoanalyst Jacques Lacan, an essentialism derived from consciousness itself in the case of Sartre.

Even so, many readers may feel that particularly in the later books of poetry up to *Ce qui fut sans lumière/In the Shadow's Light*, Bonnefoy's quasi transcendental affirmations of faith seem to have the effect of dissolving the need for poetic variety and poetic struggle. Such affirmations may have the effect of bringing to an end the rhythm and the forward motion of any one book as a whole, features that are characteristic of Bonnefoy's best output. Or perhaps it is a certain valedictory, portentous quality in some of the writing that might alienate some readers. We may feel that we are being asked to accept that in the here and now of word and verse, some of the great imponderables of existence are being resolved.

Let me randomly, and brutally, take some examples. The last section or chapter of *Pierre écrite/Written Stone* (1965) is called *Le dialogue d'angoisse et de désir/The Dialogue of Anguish and Desire*. The second poem there ends with a couplet that takes the form of a statement (this is Richard Pevear's translation):

> The iron of warring words subsides
> In the happy stream of matter.

We might counter that the potential violence of words and their manipulation is not to be so simply undone, and that writers who wish to make this attempt do so with more urgency and more drama when working as though their goal were perpetually, almost by definition, beyond their reach.

Another example. One of the chapters of *Dans le Leurre du Seuil/ The Lure of the Threshold* (1975) is called *La Terre/The Earth*. Several stanzas in this long, continuous composition begin 'I cry, Look', or 'I cry, Listen'. Each time, we are asked to look in front of us at earthly, elemental features – light, fire, an almond-tree, a grain of salt – or to listen out for, say, music that has suddenly stopped. The epigraph at the head of this collection is a quotation from *A Winter's Tale*: 'They looked as they had heard of a world ransom'd, or one destroyed.'

In Bonnefoy's book, destruction has an almost educational or visionary force – it acts to rip the scales from our eyes. The 'Look', the 'Listen' are exhortations to confront afresh the simplicity of being, the self-evidence of our contact with what is tactile and human. But we might be provoked into thinking that simplicity needs more conquering than this. We might insist that a simple speech act, or a simple rhetoric of indication, are not enough to immerse us in a simplicity of thought and response. For the same reason, we may remain unmoved by the thunderous 'Yes' which opens several stanzas in a row in the section called *L'Epars, l'indivisible/ The Scattered, The Indivisible* of the same book. Such a ploy may seem like rather a hollow attempt, taking us back to Victor Hugo, at affirming complex speculations such as the following: ancient aspiration made flesh in present images; mere appearance given temporality and depth by the sensations produced by colour...

How different such a writing is from that of many other postwar French poets. How different from René Char's *Les Matinaux/ The Dawn Breakers* of 1949, published four years earlier than *Douve* – from Char's own pursuit of simplicity, and of a tangible sense of being on earth, through tense and violent aphoristic writing. How different also from Henri Michaux's project as a writer. This is an aggressive involvement, expressed in still new form one last time in his last book *Déplacements dégagements / Spaced, Displaced* of 1984, with any experience, however frustrating or painful, with any fantasy, however violent, that might allow Michaux to construct intimations of the unorthodox, of the untreatable, of the *new* beyond the merely novel.

It is not my purpose in this coda to dictate ways of responding to the affirmative mode in Bonnefoy's poetry, or to suggest ways in which it might be related to what Bonnefoy is seeking more generally to achieve as a poet. I would like simply to emphasise the dangers inherent in taking any piece of writing by Bonnefoy out of context, as I have done just now. It is precisely to avert such potential misrepresentation that *Douve*, like the other works in this series (which include the volumes by Char and Michaux mentioned above), is published here in its entirety. Perhaps it is also true that confident affirmation is more a feature of the books published between *Douve* and *In the Shadow's Light* than it is of the others. Let me also point out again the reversible ways, as it were, in which many of Bonnefoy's individual poems, from any of the books, can be read – for example the one of many 'A Voice' poems in *Douve* I discussed earlier. And finally, I think Bonnefoy's work is perhaps at its most exciting when considered as an interactive whole comprising poetry and essays.

I am thinking now of the *Récits en rêve/ Stories in dream*, published in 1987, and in particular of the piece called 'L'Arrière-pays'/'Hinterland', first published in 1972. I can think of no other moment where Bonnefoy's apprehension of place is more *textual*, more deftly aware of the fragility of its own circumference and scope. At the same time, Bonnefoy's sinuous, meditative remembering here, the shifting yet limpid qualities of his syntax, allow passages between ideas and sensations which give a kind of subjective depth to his thinking. The opening paragraph takes the paradigmatic notion of a crossroads, alters it by saying that neither choice can be fulfilling in itself, since the other will always hold more unpredictable instances of coming upon sense, upon on a sense of purpose and meaning, that would be provoked by the configurations of the land over there. Typically, the features of landscape which Bonnefoy evokes entwine the natural and the cultural: the silhouette of mountain tops, water, the façade of a church. As the ancient story of the Cretan liar suggests, there may always be some doubt about whether we have been encouraged to take the right turning: perhaps any expert opinion about the lie of the land might turn out to be a deception. Bonnefoy takes this on explicitly here, in fact a decision about right and wrong, here at this crossroads, would involve a detachment from the those paths which Bonnefoy seeks to uncover, and which lead suddenly from image to its depth, and from culture to its living temporality. These paths are *imagined* here by Bonnefoy, and the provisional quality which results from this, together with the onus it places on the reader to be involved in the text, is what gives Bonnefoy's notion of place its strength. It is a strength in 'virtuality', a confidence in reading *through* surfaces. This a confidence to see beyond the surfaces of what is presented to us in geographical, ideological or aesthetic forms. But equally, this is a relishing in the chance twists and turns which such forms and surfaces display, and through which they change the direction of our thought. Bonnefoy's 'virtuality' is a savouring of Proustian inroads into a subjective sense of *existing* as a body in time and in culture. Bonnefoy's writing is an invitation to dive from a 'balcony' of lucid knowledge and detachment into the waters of what we might become, and to come up air covered in the 'seaweed' of our becoming. It is an invitation that is filled by engagements with texts.

Either with 'Hinterland', or other texts, verbal or visual. In 'Hinterland', Bonnefoy engages suggestively with the interplay of surface and depth characteristic of Paolo Ucello's mysterious fascination with perspective; with the 'non-conceptual clairvoyance' of Nicholas Poussin's use of blue. He might also have worked in some thoughts on Poussin's contemporary, Claude le Lorrain. One of his best known pictures – *The Enchanted Castle* (or *Landscape with Psyche outside the Palace of Cupid*, 1664) – is reproduced on the cover of this book. Bonnefoy writes a poem in response to looking at this painting, and it is included in his penultimate book of verse *Ce qui fut sans lumière/In the Shadow's Light*, published in 1987. Lorrain's blue is not as bright or as sharp as Poussin's, and yet it often has a depth all its own made up, paradoxically, of the thinness with which the paint seems to be applied. In this way, Lorrain's blue seems to evoke horizons with a paradoxical, risky and fascinating combination of deftness and provisionality.

In his poem responding to the picture, Bonnefoy expresses an anxiety about whether such painting does not have the effect of intensifying the transience and the corruptibility of bodily existence. But the poem is also a tribute to Lorrain's honesty in working in that perpetually mobile space in between constructing and ruin. In the picture, culture, suggesting construction, the spectre of experience processed in ideological packages, is present in the form of Cupid's Castle, and the Neo-Classical style it shares with the posture of Psyche in the foreground. Psyche and the Castle of her dreams are both placed within a specific moment in historical time, a specific perception of the past – of Classical Antiquity – and a specific appeal to it. And yet it is this very placing which seems to allow for a resistance to such packaging, or rather for a further delving into it, for a kind of pictorial kneading of Psyche's desire. She and the Castle are almost lost in the natural setting which overshadows them. But nature on the one hand, and the human and the human-made on the other, are each made present in the picture by the same Neo-Classical style and its impact. And yet *within* this impact, a diversity of images is produced in the picture; there is tension between woman and nature, but also mobility, a mysterious indecisiveness about their interaction. The picture seems to send out an invitation to imagine culture, social interaction, desire, all in a state of becoming. Is Psyche waiting for Cupid, or already abandoned by him, betrayed by her sisters? The picture delivers no clues. But in that place of art and text, a place perpetually in between construction and ruin, in between fulfilment and catastrophe, Bonnefoy seeks to take a step forward – to weave dreams, perhaps, that allow for their own unwinding and scattering.

TIMOTHY MATHEWS
Trinity Hall, Cambridge

Bibliography: Works mentioned and further reading

YVES BONNEFOY: Poetry

Poèmes: comprising *Du mouvement et de l'immobilité de Douve; Hier régnant désert; Pierre écrite, Dans le Leurre du Seuil* (Paris: Mercure de France, 1978; and with a preface by Jean Starobinski (Paris: Poésie/Gallimard, 1982).

Ce qui fut sans lumière (Paris: Mercure de France, 1987).

Début et fin de la neige, suivi de *Là où retombe la flèche* (Paris: Mercure de France, 1991).

Poems 1959-1975, a translation by Richard Pevear of *Pierre écrite* [*Written Stone*] and *Dans le Leurre du Seuil* [*The Lure of the Threshold*] (New York: Vintage Books, 1985).

Early Poems 1947-1959, translated by Galway Kinnell & Richard Pevear (Athens, Ohio: Ohio University Press, 1991).

Ce qui fut sans lumière [*In the Shadow's Light*], translated by John T. Naughton, with an interview with Yves Bonnefoy and John T. Naughton (Chicago & London: Chicago University Press, 1991).

Yves Bonnefoy: Recent Work, supplement ed. Anthony Rudolf, *Modern Poetry in Translation,* new series: 1 (King's College, London, 1992).

YVES BONNEFOY: Critical books and essays

Arthur Rimbaud (Paris: Seuil, 1961).

L'Improbable, suivi d'*Un rêve fait à Mantoue* (Paris: Mercure de France, 1980; Gallimard, collection Idées, 1983).

Dictionnaire des mythologies et des religions des sociétés traditionelles et du monde antique, sous la direction de Yves Bonnefoy (Paris: Flammarion, 1981); *Mythologies,* ed. Yves Bonnefoy, translated by W. Doniger (Chicago & London: Chicago University Press, 1991).

Entretiens sur la poésie (Neuchâtel: La Baconnière, 1982).

La Présence et l'Image (Paris: Mercure de France, 1983).

Récits en rêves (Paris: Mercure de France, 1987).

La Vérité de parole (Paris, Mercure de France, 1988).

Un autre époque de l'écriture (Paris: Mercure de France, 1988).

Sur un sculpteur et des peintres (Paris: Plon, 1989).

The Act and The Place of Poetry, selected essays in translation, edited with an introduction by John T. Naughton, and with a foreword by Joseph Frank (Chicago & London: Chicago University Press, 1989).

Giacometti (Paris: Flammarion, 1991); available in English translated by Jean Stewart, distributed by Thames & Hudson.

YVES BONNEFOY: Translations

Hamlet, King Lear, with 'Readiness, Ripeness: *Hamlet, King Lear* (Paris: Gallimard, Collection Folio, 1978).

Quarante-cinq poèmes de Yeats, with 'Resurrection', with introduction and notes (Paris: Hermann, 1989).

Critical Books on Yves Bonnefoy and other writers

Mary Ann Caws: *Yves Bonnefoy* (Boston: Twayne Publishers, 1984).

John E. Jackson: *La Question du moi – un aspect de la moderné poétique européenne: T.S. Eliot, Paul Celan, Yves Bonnefoy* (Neuchâtel: La Baconnière, 1978).

John T. Naughton: *The Poetics of Yves Bonnefoy* (Chicago & London: Chicago University Press, 1984).

Richard Stamelman: *Lost Beyond Telling: representations of death and absence in modern French poetry* (Ithaca & London, Cornell University Press, 1990).

Jérôme Thélot: *Poétique d'Yves Bonnefoy* (Geneva: Droz, 1983).

Other works mentioned

Roland Barthes: *Le Degré zéro de l'écriture* (Paris: Seuil, 1953); *Writing Degree Zero and Elements of Semiology*, translated by Annette Lavers and Colin Smith (London: Cape, 1967).

——: *S/Z* (Paris: Seuil, 1970); *S/Z*, translated by Richard Miller (Oxford: Blackwell, 1990).

——: *Le Plaisir du texte* (Paris: Seuil, 1973); *The Pleasure of the Text*, translated by Richard Miller (Oxford: Blackwell, 1990).

——: *Roland Barthes* (Paris: Seuil, 1975); *Roland Barthes*, translated by Richard Howard (London: Macmillan, 1977).

——: *Leçon* (Paris: Seuil, 1973); *Inaugural Lecture*, in *Selected Writings*, translated and edited with an introduction by Susan Sontag (London: Fontana Pocket Readers, 1983).

——: *Fragments d'un discours amoureux* (Paris: Seuil, 1977); *Fragments of a Lover's Discourse*, translated by Richard Howard (London: Cape, 1979).

——: *La Chambre claire* (Paris: Gallimard, 1980); *Camera Lucida*, translated by Richard Howard (London: Flamingo, 1984).

R.M. Hare: *Plato*, Past Masters (Oxford University Press, 1982).

Jean-Paul Sartre: *L'Imaginaire* (Paris: Gallimard, 1940, and in collection Idées).

NOTE: Unless otherwise stated, all translations in the Introduction, except those from *Douve*, are by Timothy Mathews.

43

Mais la vie de l'esprit ne s'effraie
point devant la mort et n'est pas celle
qui s'en garde pure. Elle est la vie qui
la supporte et se maintient en elle.

HEGEL

But the life of the spirit
is not frightened at death
and does not keep itself pure
of it. It endures death
and maintains itself in it.

HEGEL

THÉÂTRE
THEATRE

I

Je te voyais courir sur des terrasses,
Je te voyais lutter contre le vent,
Le froid saignait sur tes lèvres.

Et je t'ai vue te rompre et jouir d'être morte ô plus belle
Que la foudre, quand elle tache les vitres blanches de ton sang.

I

I saw you running on the terraces,
I saw you fight against the wind,
The coldness bled on your lips.

And I have seen you break and rejoice at being dead – O more
    beautiful
Than the lightning, when it stains the white windowpanes of your
    blood.

II

L'été vieillissant te gerçait d'un plaisir monotone, nous méprisions l'ivresse imparfaite de vivre.

«Plutôt le lierre, disais-tu, l'attachement du lierre aux pierres de sa nuit: présence sans issue, visage sans racine.

«Dernière vitre heureuse que l'ongle solaire déchire, plutôt dans la montagne ce village où mourir.

«Plutôt ce vent...»

II

The dying summer had chapped you with listless pleasure, we felt only scorn for the marred joys of living.

'Rather ivy,' you would say, 'the way it clings to the stones of its night: presence without exit, face without roots.

'Last radiant windowpane ripped by the sun's claw, rather in the mountains this village to die in.

'Rather this wind...'

III

Il s'agissait d'un vent plus fort que nos mémoires,
Stupeur des robes et cri des rocs – et tu passais devant ces flammes
La tête quadrillée les mains fendues et toute
En quête de la mort sur les tambours exultants de tes gestes.

C'était jour de tes seins
Et tu régnais enfin absente de ma tête.

III

It was a wind stronger than our memories,
Stupor of clothing and cry of rocks – and you moved in front of
    those flames,
Head graphlined, hands split open, all
Bent on death on the exulting drums of your gestures.

It was day of your breasts:
And you reigned at last absent from my head.

IV

Je me réveille, il pleut. Le vent te pénètre, Douve, lande rési-
neuse endormie près de moi. Je suis sur une terrasse, dans un trou
de la mort. De grands chiens de feuillages tremblent.

Le bras que tu soulèves, soudain, sur une porte, m'illumine à
travers les âges. Village de braise, à chaque instant je te vois naître,
Douve,

À chaque instant mourir.

IV

I awaken, it is raining. The wind pierces you, Douve, resinous
heath sleeping near me. I am on a terrace, in a pit of death. Great
dogs of leaves tremble.

The arm you lift, suddenly, at a doorway, lights me across the
ages. Village of embers, each instant I see you being born, Douve,

Each instant dying.

V

Le bras que l'on soulève et le bras que l'on tourne
Ne sont d'un même instant que pour nos lourdes têtes,
Mais rejetés ces draps de verdure et de boue
Il ne reste qu'un feu du royaume de mort.

La jambe demeublée où le grand vent pénètre
Poussant devant lui des têtes de pluie
Ne vous éclairera qu'au seuil de ce royaume,
Gestes de Douve, gestes déjà plus lents, gestes noirs.

V

The arm lifted and the arm turned
Are simultaneous only for our dull wits,
But these sheets of greenness and mud thrown back,
What is left is a fire in death's kingdom.

The dismantled leg which the high wind pierces
Driving heads of rain before it
Will only light you to the threshold of that kingdom,
Douve's hands, hands already slower, dark hands.

VI

Quelle pâleur te frappe, rivière souterraine, quelle artère en toi se rompt, où l'écho retentit de ta chute?

Ce bras que tu soulèves soudain s'ouvre, s'enflamme. Ton visage recule. Quelle brume croissante m'arrache ton regard? Lente falaise d'ombre, frontière de la mort.

Des bras muets t'accueillent, arbres d'une autre rive.

VI

What paleness comes over you, underground river, what artery breaks in you, where your fall echoes?

This arm you lift suddenly opens, catches fire. Your face draws back. What thickening mist wrenches your eye from mine? Slow cliffs of shadow, frontier of death.

Mute arms reach for you, trees of another shore.

VII

Blessée confuse dans les feuilles,
Mais prise par le sang de pistes qui se perdent,
Complice encor du vivre.

Je t'ai vue ensablée au terme de ta lutte
Hésiter aux confins du silence et de l'eau,
Et la bouche souillée des dernières étoiles
Rompre d'un cri l'horreur de veiller dans ta nuit.

Ô dressant dans l'air dur soudain comme une roche
Un beau geste de houille.

VII

Wounded, lost among the leaves,
But gripped by the blood of vanishing paths,
Accomplice yet of life.

I have seen you, sunk down at struggle's end,
Falter at the edge of silence and water,
And mouth sullied by the last stars
Break with a cry the horrible nightwatch.

O raising into the air suddenly hard as rock
A bright gesture of coal.

VIII

La musique saugrenue commence dans les mains, dans les genoux, puis c'est la tête qui craque, la musique s'affirme sous les lèvres, sa certitude pénètre le versant souterrain du visage.

À présent se disloquent les menuiseries faciales. À présent l'on procède à l'arrachement de la vue.

VIII

The weird music starts in the hands, in the knees, then it is the head that cracks, the music declares itself under the lips, it surges across the underslope of the face.

Now the woodwork of the face comes apart. Now begins the tearing out of the sight.

IX

Blanche sous un plafond d'insectes, mal éclairée, de profil
Et ta robe tachée du venin des lampes,
Je te découvre étendue,
Ta bouche plus haute qu'un fleuve se brisant au loin sur la terre.

Être défait que l'être invincible rassemble,
Présence ressaisie dans la torche du froid,
Ô guetteuse toujours je te découvre morte,
Douve disant Phénix je veille dans ce froid.

IX

White under a ceiling of insects, poorly lit, in profile,
Your dress stained by the venom of lamps,
I find you stretched out,
Your mouth higher than a river breaking far away on the earth.

Broken being the unconquerable being reassembles,
Presence seized again in the torch of cold,
O watcher always I find you dead,
Douve saying Phoenix I wake in this cold.

X

Je vois Douve étendue. Au plus haut de l'espace charnel je l'entends bruire. Les princes-noirs hâtent leurs mandibules à travers cet espace où les mains de Douve se développent, os défaits de leur chair se muant en toile grise que l'araignée massive éclaire.

X

I see Douve stretched out. On the highest level of fleshly space I hear her rustling. Black-princes hurry their mandibles across that space where Douve's hands unfold, unfleshed bones becoming a grey web which the huge spider lights.

XI

Couverte de l'humus silencieux du monde,
Parcourue des rayons d'une araignée vivante,
Déjà soumise au devenir du sable
Et tout écartelée secrète connaissance.

Parée pour une fête dans le vide
Et les dents découvertes comme pour l'amour,

Fontaine de ma mort présente insoutenable.

XI

Covered by the world's silent humus,
Webbed through by a living spider's rays,
Already undergoing the life and death of sand
And splayed out secret knowledge.

Adorned for a festival in the void,
Teeth bared as if for love,

Fountain of my death living unbearable.

XII

Je vois Douve étendue. Dans la ville écarlate de l'air, où combattent les branches sur son visage, où des racines trouvent leur chemin dans son corps – elle rayonne une joie stridente d'insectes, une musique affreuse.

Au pas noir de la terre, Douve ravagée, exultante, rejoint la lampe noueuse des plateaux.

XII

I see Douve stretched out. In the scarlet city of air, where branches clash across her face, where roots find their way into her body – she radiates a strident insect joy, a frightful music.

With the black tread of earth, Douve, ravaged, exultant, returns to the highlands, this lamp.

XIII

Ton visage ce soir éclairé par la terre,
Mais je vois tes yeux se corrompre
Et le mot visage n'a plus de sens.

La mer intérieure éclairée d'aigles tournants,
Ceci est une image.
Je te détiens froide à une profondeur où les images ne prennent plus.

XIII

Your face tonight lighted by the earth,
But I see your eyes' corruption
And the word face makes no sense.

The inner sea lighted by turning eagles,
This is an image.
I hold you cold at a depth where images will not take.

XIV

Je vois Douve étendue. Dans une pièce blanche, les yeux cernés de plâtre, bouche vertigineuse et les mains condamnées à l'herbe luxuriante qui l'envahit de toutes parts.

La porte s'ouvre. Un orchestre s'avance. Et des yeux à facettes, des thorax pelucheux, des têtes froides à becs, à mandibules, l'inondent.

XIV

I see Douve stretched out. In a white room, eyes circled with plaster, mouth towering, hands condemned to the lush grass entering her from all sides.

The door opens. An orchestra surges forward. And faceted eyes, woolly thoraxes, cold heads beaked and pincered, flood over her.

XV

Ô douée d'un profil où s'acharne la terre
Je te vois disparaître.

L'herbe nue sur tes lèvres et l'éclat du silex
Inventent ton dernier sourire,

Science profonde où se calcine
Le vieux bestiaire cérébral.

XV

O gifted with a profile where earth rages,
I see you disappear.

On your lips bare grass and flintsparks
Invent your last smile,

Deep knowledge which burns to ashes
The old bestiary of the mind.

60

XVI

Demeure d'un feu sombr où convergent nos pentes! Sous ses voûtes je te vois luire, Douve immobile, prise dans le filet vertical de la mort.

Douve géniale, renversée: au pas des soleils dans l'espace funèbre, elle accède lentement aux étages inférieurs.

XVI

Home of a dark fire where our slopes converge! Under its vaults I see you glimmer, Douve, motionless, caught in the vertical net of death.

Immaterial Douve, overturned: with the march of suns through funeral space, she reaches slowly the lower levels.

XVII

Le ravin pénètre dans la bouche maintenant,
Les cinq doigts se dispersent en hasards de forêt maintenant,
La tête première coule entre les herbes maintenant,
La gorge se farde de neige et de loups maintenant,
Les yeux ventent sur quels passagers de la mort et c'est nous dans
  ce vent dans cette eau dans ce foid maintenant.

XVII

The ravine enters the mouth now,
The five fingers scatter in the forest now,
The primal head flows out among the grasses now,
The throat paints itself with snow and wolves now,
The eyes blow on which of death's passengers and it is we in this
  wind in this water in this cold now.

XVIII

Présence exacte qu'aucune flamme désormais ne saurait restreindre; convoyeuse du froid secret; vivante, de ce sang qui renaît et s'accroît où se déchire le poème,

Il fallait qu'ainsi tu parusses aux limites sourdes, et d'un site funèbre où ta lumière empire, que tu subisses l'épreuve.

Ô plus belle et la mort infuse dans ton rire! J'ose à présent te rencontrer, je soutiens l'éclat de tes gestes.

XVIII

Exact presence whom no flame can ever again hold back; attendant of the secret cold; living, by that blood which springs and flourishes there where the poem is torn,

It was necessary for you to appear, thus, at the numb limits, to undergo this ordeal, this death-land where your light increases.

O more beautiful, with death-steeped laughter! Now I dare meet you, now I can face your gestures' flashing.

XIX

Au premier jour du froid notre tête s'évade
Comme un prisonnier fuit dans l'ozone majeur,
Mais Douve d'un instant cette flèche retombe
Et brise sur le sol les palmes de sa tête.

Ainsi avions-nous cru réincarner nos gestes,
Mais la tête niée nous buvons une eau froide,
Et des liasses de mort pavoisent ton sourire,
Ouverture tentée dans l'épaisseur du monde.

XIX

On the first day of cold the head escapes
As a prisoner flees into rarest air,
But Douve for an instant that arrow falls
And breaks its crown of palms on the ground.

So we had dreamed of incarnate gestures
But with mind cancelled we drink a cold water,
And death's banners flutter at your smile,
Attempted rift in the thickness of the world.

DERNIERS GESTES
LAST ACTS

Aux Arbres

Vous qui vous êtes effacés sur son passage,
Qui avez refermé sur elle vos chemins,
Impassibles garants que Douve même morte
Sera lumière encore n'étant rien.

Vous fibreuse matière et densité,
Arbres, proches de moi quand elle s'est jetée
Dans la barque des morts et la bouche serrée
Sur l'obole de faim, de froid et de silence.

J'entends à travers vous quel dialogue elle tente
Avec les chiens, avec l'informe nautonier,
Et je vous appartiens par son cheminement
À travers tant de nuit et malgré tout ce fleuve.

Le tonnerre profond qui roule sur vos branches,
Les fêtes qu'il enflamme au sommet de l'été
Signifient qu'elle lie sa fortune à la mienne
Dans la médiation de votre austérité.

To the Trees

You who stepped aside as she passed,
Who closed over your pathways behind her,
Stolid bondsmen for Douve: that even dead
She will again be light, being nothing.

You fibrous matter and density,
Trees, close to me when she leapt
Into the boat of the dead, mouth shut tight
On the obolus of hunger, of silence, of cold.

Through you I hear the dialogue she tries
With the dogs, with the misshapen oarsman,
And I become part of you as she travels
Through so much night in spite of all this river.

The deep thunder rolling on your branches,
The festivals it ignites at the peak of summer
Mean that she binds her destiny to mine
Through the mediation of your austerity.

Que saisir sinon qui s'échappe,
Que voir sinon qui s'obscurcit,
Que désirer sinon qui meurt,
Sinon qui parle et se déchire?

Parole proche de moi
Que chercher sinon ton silence,
Quelle lueur sinon profonde
Ta conscience ensevelie,

Parole jetée matérielle
Sur l'origine et la nuit?

What shall I seize but what escapes,
What shall I see but what fades,
What shall I desire but what dies,
But what speaks and tears itself?

Speech close to me,
What shall I see but your silence,
What gleam but deep down
Your buried consciousness,

Speech material span
Over origin and night?

Le Seul Temoin

I

Ayant livré sa tête aux basses flammes
De la mer, ayant perdu ses mains
Dans son anxieuse profondeur, ayant jeté
Aux matières de l'eau sa chevelure;
Étant morte, puisque mourir est ce chemin
De verticalité sous la lumière,
Et ivre encore étant morte: ô je fus,
Ménade consumée, dure joie mais perfide,
Le seul témoin, la seule bête prise
Dans ces rets de ta mort que furent sables
Ou rochers ou chaleur, ton signe disais-tu.

II

Elle fuit vers les saules; le sourire
Des arbres l'enveloppe, simulant
La joie simple d'un jeu. Mais la lumière
Est sombre sur ses mains de suppliante,
Et le feu vient laver sa face, emplir sa bouche
Et rejeter son corps dans le gouffre des saules.

Ô t'abîmant du flanc de la table osirienne
Dans les eaux de la mort!
Une dernière fois de tes seins
Éclairant les convives.
Mais répandant le jour de ta tête glacée
Sur la stérilité des sites infernaux.

Sole Witness

I

Having given her head to the low flames
Of the sea, having lost her hands
In its restless depths, having thrown
Her hair to the elements of water;
Being dead, since dying is this road
Of verticality under the light,
And drunken, still, in death: I was,
O Maenad in ashes, hard but perfidious joy,
The sole witness, the only beast caught
In those nets of your death which were sand
Or rocks or heat, your sign you used to say.

II

She runs toward the willows; the smile
Of the trees closes round her, feigning
The simple joy of some game. But the light
Is dark on her supplicating hands,
And fire comes to wash her face, fill her mouth,
Throw back her body deep among the willows.

O plunging from the side of the Osirian feast
Into the waters of death!
A last time with your breasts
Lighting the partakers.
But shedding the light of your frozen head
On the sterility of the hellish shores.

III

Le peu d'espace entre l'arbre et le seuil
Suffit pour que tu t'élances encore et que tu meures
Et que je croie revivre à la lumière
D'ombrages que tu fus.

Et que j'oublie
Ton visage criant sur chaque mur,
Ô Ménade peut-être réconciliée
Avec tant d'ombre heureuse sur la pierre.

IV

Es-tu vraiment morte ou joues-tu
Encore à simuler la pâleur et le sang,
Ô toi passionnément au sommeil qui te livres
Comme on ne sait que mourir?

Es-tu vraiment morte ou joues-tu
Encore en tout miroir
À perdre ton reflet, ta chaleur et ton sang
Dans l'obscurcissement d'un visage immobile?

III

The gap between the tree and the threshold
Is enough for you to rush out again and to die
And for me to think I live again in the light
Of the shadows you used to be.

And for me to forget
Your face shouting on every wall,
O Maenad reconciled perhaps
With so much shadow happy on the stone.

IV

Are you really dead or do you still play
At imitating that paleness and that blood,
You, oh passionately giving yourself to sleep
In the way only used for dying?

Are you really dead or do you still play
In every mirror
At losing your reflection, your warmth, your blood,
In the darkening of a motionless face?

V

Où maintenant est le cerf qui témoigna
Sous ces arbres de justice,
Qu'une route de sang par elle fut ouverte,
Un silence nouveau par elle inventé.

Portant sa robe comme lac de sable, comme froid,
Comme cerf pourchassé aux lisières,
Qu'elle mourut, portant sa robe la plus belle,
Et d'une terre vipérine revenue?

VI

Sur un fangeux hiver, Douve, j'étendais
Ta face lumineuse et basse de forêt.
Tout se défait, pensai-je, tout s'éloigne.

Je te revis violente et riant sans retour,
De tes cheveux au soir d'opulentes saisons
Dissimuler l'éclat d'un visage livide.

Je te revis furtive. En lisière des arbres
Paraître comme un feu quand l'automne resserre
Tout le bruit de l'orage au cœur des frondaisons.

Ô plus noire et déserte! Enfin je te vis morte,
Inapaisable éclair que le néant supporte,
Vitre sitôt éteinte, et d'obscure maison.

V

Where now is the stag who testified
Under these trees of justice
That she opened a roadway of blood,
That she invented a new silence.

That in her dress as if some lake of sand, or cold,
Or stag hunted into the fringes,
She died, in her most beautiful dress,
Returned from a poisonous land?

VI

Over a muddy winter, Douve, I spread out
Your face, luminous and low, like a forest.
Everything dies, I thought, everything vanishes.

I saw you, violent, helplessly laughing,
At the fall of opulent seasons, hiding
With your hair the glare of a livid face.

And I saw you furtive. At the trees' edge
Appearing like a fire when the autumn draws
The whole noise of the storm to the heart of leaves.

O blackest and most barren! At last I saw you dead,
Unappeasable lightning-bolt strung out on the void,
Window now put out, and of a dark house.

Vrai Nom

Je nommerai désert ce château que tu fus,
Nuit cette voix, absence ton visage,
Et quand tu tomberas dans la terre stérile
Je nommerai néant l'éclair qui t'a porté.

Mourir est un pays que tu aimais. Je viens
Mais éternellement par tes sombres chemins.
Je détruis ton désir, ta forme, ta mémoire,
Je suis ton ennemi qui n'aura de pitié.

Je te nommerai guerre et je prendrai
Sur toi les libertés de la guerre et j'aurai
Dans mes mains ton visage obscur et traversé,
Dans mon cœur ce pays qu'illumine l'orage.

True Name

I will name wilderness the castle which you were,
Night your voice, absence your face,
And when you fall back into sterile earth
I will name nothingness the lightning which bore you.

Dying is a country which you loved. I approach
Along your dark ways, but eternally.
I destroy your desire, your form, your trace in me,
I am your enemy who shows no mercy.

I will name you war and I will take
With you the liberties of war, and I will have
In my hands your dark-crossed face,
In my heart this land which the storm lights.

La lumiere profonde a besoin pour paraître
D'une terre rouée et craquante de nuit.
C'est d'un bois ténébreux que la flamme s'exalte.
Il faut à la parole même une matière,
Un inerte rivage au delà de tout chant.

Il te faudra franchir la mort pour que tu vives,
La plus pure présence est un sang répandu.

If it is to appear, the deep light needs
A ravaged soil cracking with night.
It is from the dark wood that the flame will leap.
Speech itself needs such substance,
A lifeless shore beyond all singing.

You will have to go through death to live,
The purest presence is blood which is shed.

Phénix

L'oiseau se portera au-devant de nos têtes,
Une épaule de sang pour lui se dressera.
Il fermera joyeux ses ailes sur le faîte
De cet arbre ton corps que tu lui offriras.

Il chantera longtemps s'éloignant dans les branches,
L'ombre viendra lever les bornes de son cri.
Refusant toute mort inscrite sur les branches
Il osera franchir les crêtes de la nuit.

Phoenix

The bird will soar to meet our heads,
A shoulder of blood will be lifted for him.
He will fold his joyful wings on the peak
Of this tree your body you will offer him.

He will sing a long time fading into the branches,
Shadows will come on the boundaries of his cry.
Refusing any death hinted by the branches
He will dare to pass the summits of the night.

Cette pierre ouverte est-ce toi, ce logis dévasté,
Comment peut-on mourir?

J'ai apporté de la lumière, j'ai cherché,
Partout régnait le sang.
Et je criais et je pleurais de tout mon corps.

This opened stone is it you, this wrecked house,
How can one die?

I brought light, I looked,
Everywhere blood reigned.
And I cried, I wept with my whole body.

Vrai Corps

Close la bouche et lavé le visage,
Purifié le corps, enseveli
Ce destin éclairant dans la terre du verbe,
Et le mariage le plus bas s'est accompli.

Tue cette voix qui criait à ma face
Que nous étions hagards et séparés,
Murés ces yeux: et je tiens Douve morte
Dans l'âpreté de soi avec moi refermée.

Et si grand soit le froid qui monte de ton être,
Si brûlant soit le gel de notre intimité,
Douve, je parle en toi; et je t'enserre
Dans l'acte de connaître et de nommer.

True Body

The mouth shut tight, the face washed,
The body purified, that shining fate
Buried in the earth of words,
And the most basic marriage is accomplished.

Silenced that voice which shouted to my face
That we were stranded and apart,
Walled up those eyes: and I hold Douve dead
In the rasping self locked with me again.

And however great the coldness rising from you,
However searing the ice of our embrace,
Douve, I do speak in you; and I clasp you
In the act of knowing and of naming.

Art poétique

Visage séparé de ses branches premières,
Beauté toute d'alarme par ciel bas,

En quel âtre dresser le feu de ton visage
Ô Ménade saisie jetée la tête en bas?

Art of Poetry

Face cut off from its first branchings,
Beauty made of alarms under a low sky,

In what hearth shall I build the fire of your face
Maenad seized and thrown head first?

DOUVE PARLE

DOUVE SPEAKS

Quelle parole a surgi près de moi,
Quel cri se fait sur une bouche absente?
À peine si j'entends crier contre moi,
À peine si je sens ce souffle qui me nomme.

Pourtant ce cri sur moi vient de moi,
Je suis muré dans mon extravagance.
Quelle divine ou quelle étrange voix
Eût consenti d'habiter mon silence?

What word springs up beside me,
What cry is forming on an absent mouth?
I hardly hear this cry against me,
I hardly feel that breath saying my name.

And yet the cry comes from myself,
I am walled up in my extravagance.
What divine or what strange voice
Would have agreed to live in my silence?

Une Voix

Quelle maison veux-tu dresser pour moi,
Quelle écriture noire quand vient le feu?

*

J'ai reculé longtemps devant tes signes,
Tu m'as chassée de toute densité.

*

Mais voici que la nuit incessante me garde,
Par de sombres chevaux je me sauve de toi.

A Voice

What house would you build for me,
What black writing when the fire comes?

*

I drew back from your signs a long time,
You hurled me from all densities.

*

But now endless night watches over me,
Through dark horses I flee from you.

Une Autre Voix

Secouant ta chevelure ou cendre de Phénix,
Quel geste tentes-tu quand tout s'arrête,

Et quand minuit dans l'être illumine les tables?

*

Quel signe gardes-tu sur tes lèvres noires,
Quelle pauvre parole quand tout se tait,

Dernier tison quand l'âtre hésite et se referme?

*

Je saurai vivre en toi, j'arracherai
En toi toute lumière,

Toute incarnation, tout récif, toute loi.

*

Et dans le vide où je te hausse j'ouvrirai
La route de la foudre,

Ou plus grand cri qu'être ait jamais tenté.

Another Voice

Shaking your hair or Phoenix's ashes,
What motion do you make when everything stops,

And the inner midnight lights the tables?

*

What sign do you keep on your black lips,
What wretched word when everything hushes,

Last brand when the hearth flickers and closes?

*

I will know how to live in you, I will
Tear every light from you,

Every incarnation, every reef, every law.

*

And where I lift you in the emptiness I will
Open the road of lightning,

Or greatest cry a man ever attempted.

Si cette nuit est autre que la nuit,
Renais, lointaine voix bénéfique, réveille
L'argile la plus grave où le grain ait dormi.
Parle: je n'étais plus que terre désirante,
Voici les mots enfin de l'aube et de la pluie.
Mais parle que je sois la terre favorable,
Parle s'il est encor un jour enseveli.

If this night be other than the night,
Come back to life, distant beneficent voice, wake
The heaviest clay in which grain ever slept.
Speak: I was nothing but yearning earth,
Now come the words of dawn and rain at last.
But speak that I may be propitious earth,
Speak if somewhere lives a buried day.

Douve Parle

I

Quelquefois, disais-tu, errante à l'aube
Sur des chemins noircis,
Je partageais l'hypnose de la pierre,
J'étais aveugle comme elle.
Or est venu ce vent par quoi mes comédies
Se sont élucidées en l'acte de mourir.

Je désirais l'été,
Un furieux été pour assécher mes larmes,
Or est venu ce froid qui grandit dans mes membres,
Et je fus éveillée et je souffris.

II

Ô fatale saison,
Ô terre la plus nue comme une lame!
Je désirais l'été,
Qui a rompu ce fer dans le vieux sang?

Vraiment je fus heureuse
À ce point de mourir.
Les yeux perdus, mes mains s'ouvrant à la souillure
D'une éternelle pluie.

Je criais, j'affrontais de ma face le vent...
Pourquoi haïr, pourquoi pleurer, j'étais vivante,
L'été profond, le jour me rassuraient.

Douve Speaks

I

Sometimes, you used to say, wandering at dawn
On blackened paths,
I shared the stone's hypnosis,
I was blind like it.
Now that wind has come by which all my games
Are given away in the act of dying.

I longed for summer,
A furious summer to dry my tears,
Now has come this coldness which swells in my flesh
And I was awakened and I suffered.

II

O fatal season,
O barest earth like a blade!
I longed for summer,
Who has broken off this sword in the old blood?

Truly I was happy
At this moment of dying.
Eyes lost, hands opening to the sullying
Of an eternal rain.

I cried out, I confronted the wind,
Why hate, why weep, I was alive,
The deep summer, the day reassured me.

III

Que le verbe s'éteigne
Sur cette face de l'être où nous sommes exposés,
Sur cette aridité que traverse
Le seul vent de finitude.

Que celui qui brûlait debout
Comme une vigne,
Que l'extrême chanteur roule de la crête
Illuminant
L'immense matière indicible.

Que le verbe s'éteigne
Dans cette pièce basse où tu me rejoins,
Que l'âtre du cri se resserre
Sur nos mots rougeoyants.

Que le froid par ma mort se lève et prenne un sens.

III

Let the word burn out
On this slope of being where we are stranded,
On this arid land
Which only the wind of our limits crosses.

Let him who burned standing up
Like a vine,
Let the wildest singer roll from the crest
Illuminating
Vast unutterable matter.

Let the word burn out
In this low room where you come to me,
Let the hearth of the cry close down
On our ember-words.

Let the cold by my death arise and take on meaning.

Demande au maître de la nuit quelle est cette nuit,
Demande: que veux-tu, ô maitre disjoint?
Naufragé de ta nuit, oui je te cherche en elle,
Je vis de tes questions, je parle dans ton sang,
Je suis le maître de ta nuit, je veille en toi comme la nuit.

Ask the master of the night what is this night,
Ask: what do you want, O master in ruins?
Shipwrecked in your night, yes I seek you in it,
I live by your questions, I speak in your blood,
I am master of your night, I wake within you like night.

Une Voix

Souviens-toi de cette île où l'on bâtit le feu
De tout olivier vif au flanc des crêtes,
Et c'est pour que la nuit soit plus haute et qu'à l'aube
Il n'y ait plus de vent que de stérilité.
Tant de chemins noircis feront bien un royaume
Où rétablir l'orgueil que nous avons été,
Car rien ne peut grandir une éternelle force
Qu'une éternelle flamme et que tout soit défait.
Pour moi je rejoindrai cette terre cendreuse,
Je coucherai mon cœur sur son corps dévasté.
Ne suis-je pas ta vie aux profondes alarmes,
Qui n'a de monument que Phénix au bûcher?

A Voice

Remember the island where they build the fire
Out of every olive tree thriving on the slopes,
In order that night should arch higher and dawn
Find no wind but in sterility.
So many charred roads will make up a kingdom
Where the pride we once knew can reign once more,
For nothing can swell an eternal force
But an eternal flame and that all be undone.
For myself I will go back to that earth of ashes,
I will lay down my heart on its ravaged body.
Am I not your life in its deepest alarms,
Whose only monument is the Phoenix's pyre?

Demande pour tes yeux que les rompe la nuit,
Rien ne commencera qu'au delà de ce voile,
Demande ce plaisir que dispense la nuit
De crier sous le cercle bas d'aucune lune,
Demande pour ta voix que l'étouffe la nuit.

Demande enfin le froid, désire cette houille.

Ask for your eyes that the night tear them,
Nothing will begin but beyond this veil,
Ask for the pleasure which the night gives,
Of crying out in this sphere of no moon,
Ask for your voice that the night muffle it.

Ask finally for cold in the darkest ore.

Une Voix

J'ai porté ma parole en vous comme une flamme,
Ténèbres plus ardues qu'aux flammes sont les vents.
Et rien ne m'a soumise en si profonde lutte,
Nulle étoile mauvaise et nul égarement.
Ainsi ai-je vécu, mais forte d'une flamme,
Qu'ai-je d'autre connu que son recourbement
Et la nuit que je sais qui viendra quand retombent
Les vitres sans destin de son élancement?
Je ne suis que parole intentée à l'absence,
L'absence détruira tout mon ressassement.
Oui, c'est bientôt périr de n'être que parole,
Et c'est tâche fatale et vain couronnement.

A Voice

I bore my words in you like a flame,
Darkness fiercer than wind on fire.
And nothing subdued me in such deep struggle,
No evil star, no stumbling from the road.
In this way I lived, strong by a flame,
What else have I known but its bending
And the night I know will come when they fall,
Those futureless windows of its first leaping.
I am nothing but words raised against absence,
Absence will destroy all my ebb and flow.
Yes, to be words only is to die out soon,
The task is doomed and its crowning vain.

Voix Basses et Phénix

UNE VOIX

Tu fus sage d'ouvrir, il vint à la nuit,
Il posa près de toi la lampe de pierre.
Il te coucha nouvelle en ta place ordinaire,
De ton regard vivant faisant étrange nuit.

UNE AUTRE VOIX

La première venue en forme d'oiseau
Frappe à ma vitre au minuit de ma veille.
J'ouvre et saisie dans sa neige tombe
Et ce logis m'échappe où je menais grand feu.

UNE VOIX

Elle gisait, le cœur découvert. À minuit,
Sous l'épais feuillage des morts,
D'une lune perdue elle devint la proie,
La maison familière où tout se rétablit.

UNE AUTRE VOIX

D'un geste il me dressa cathédrale de froid,
Ô Phénix! Cime affreuse des arbres crevassée
Par le gel! Je roulais comme torche jetée
Dans la nuit même où le Phénix se recompose.

Low Voices and Phoenix

A VOICE

You were right to open, he came by night,
He placed the stone lamp beside you.
He laid you down remade in your usual place,
Turning your living gaze into strange night.

ANOTHER VOICE

The first to arrive in the shape of a bird
Raps at my window in the midnight of my waiting.
I open and caught in its snow I fall
And the house vanishes where I lit great fires.

A VOICE

She was lying there, her heart bared. At midnight,
Under the thick foliage of the dead,
She became the prey of a wandering moon,
The familiar house where all begins again.

ANOTHER VOICE

With one motion he turned me cathedral of cold,
O Phoenix! Frightful summit of trees riven
By ice! And I fell end over end like a torch hurled
Into that very night where Phoenix re-forms.

Mais que se taise celle qui veille encor
Sur l'âtre, son visage étant chu dans les flammes,
Qui reste encore assise, étant sans corps.

Qui parle pour moi, ses lèvres étant fermées,
Qui se lève et m'appelle, étant sans chair,
Qui part laissant sa tête dessinée,

Qui rit toujours, en rire étant morte jadis.

But let her be silent, the one still keeping watch
At the hearth, her face having fallen in the flames,
Who yet remains seated, being bodiless.

Who speaks for me, her lips being shut,
Who gets up and calls me, being without flesh,
Who goes away leaving her head half-sketched,

Who laughs still, in laughter dead long since.

Tais-toi puisqu'aussi bien nous sommes de la nuit
Les plus informes souches gravitantes,
Et matière lavée et retournant aux vieilles
Idées retentissantes où le feu s'est tari,
Et face ravinée d'une aveugle présence
Avec tout feu chassée servante d'un logis,
Et parole vécue mais infiniment morte
Quand la lumière enfin s'est faite vent et nuit.

Be still for it is true we are the most
Shapeless of night's gravitating roots,
Washed matter turning again to the old
Resounding archetypes whose fire has withered,
And ravaged face of a blind presence,
Servant driven with the fire from the house,
And word that has been lived but infinitely dead
Now that the light has turned to wind and dark at last.

L'ORANGERIE
THE ORANGERY

Ainsi marcherons-nous sur les ruines d'un ciel immense,
Le site au loin s'accomplira
Comme un destin dans la vive lumière.

Le pays le plus beau longtemps cherché
S'étendra devant nous terre des salamandres.

Regarde, diras-tu, cette pierre:
Elle porte la présence de la mort.
Lampe secrète c'est elle qui brûle sous nos gestes,
Ainsi marchons-nous éclairés.

So we will walk on the ruins of a vast sky,
The far-off landscape will bloom
Like a destiny in the vivid light.

The long-sought most beautiful country
Will lie before us land of salamanders.

Look, you will say, at this stone:
Death shines from it.
Secret lamp it is this that burns under our steps,
Thus we walk lighted.

Hic est Locus Patriae

Le ciel trop bas pour toi se déchirait, les arbres
Envahissaient l'espace de ton sang.
Ainsi d'autres armées sont venues, ô Cassandre,
Et rien n'a pu survivre à leur embrassement.

Un vase décorait le seuil. Contre son marbre
Celui qui revenait sourit en s'appuyant.
Ainsi le jour baissait sur le lieudit *Aux Arbres*.
C'était jour de parole et ce fut nuit de vent.

Hic est Locus Patriae

The sky too low for you had ripped, the trees
Invaded the space of your blood.
Thus other armies came, O Cassandra,
And nothing could survive their embrace.

A vase adorned the threshold. Leaning
On its marble the one who was returning smiled.
Thus the day was dimming on the place called *The Trees*.
It had been day of words and it was night of wind.

Le lieu était désert, le sol sonore et vacant,
La clé, facile dans la porte.
Sous les arbres du parc,
Qui allait vivre en telle brume chancelait.

L'orangerie,
Nécessaire repos qu'il rejoignait,
Parut, un peu de pierre dans les branches.

Ô terre d'un destin! Une première salle
Criait de feuille morte et d'abandon.
Sur la seconde et la plus grande, la lumière
S'étendait, nappe rouge et grise, vrai bonheur.

The place was deserted, the ground ringing and empty,
The key, easy in the door.
Under the trees in the park
He who would live in that mist went staggering.

The orangery,
Necessary resting-place where he returned,
Came into view, a bit of stone between branches.

Land of his destiny! A first room
Cried out of dead leaves and dereliction.
On the second and largest the light
Spread, cloth of red and grey, true happiness.

La Salamandre

I

Et maintenant tu es Douve dans la dernière chambre d'été.

Une salamandre fuit sur le mur. Sa douce tête d'homme répand la mort de l'été. «Je veux m'abîmer en toi, vie étroite, crie Douve. Éclair vide, cours sur mes lèvres, pénètre-moi!

«J'aime m'aveugler, me livrer à la terre. J'aime ne plus savoir quelles dents froides me possèdent.»

II

Toute une nuit je t'ai rêvée ligneuse, Douve, pour mieu t'offrir à la flamme. Et statue verte épousée par l'écorce, pour mieux jouir de ta tête éclairante.

Éprouvant sous mes doigts le débat du brasier et des lèvres: je te voyais me sourire. Or, ce grand jour en toi des braises m'aveuglait.

III

«Regarde-moi, regarde-moi, j'ai couru!»

Je suis près de toi, Douve, je t'éclaire. Il n'y a plus entre nous que cette lampe rocailleuse, ce peu d'ombre apaisé, nos mains que l'ombre attend. Salamandre surprise, tu demeures immobile.

Ayant vécu l'instant où la chair la plus proche se mue en connaissance.

The Salamander

I

And now you are Douve in the last room of summer.

A salamander darts on the wall. Its gentle human head gives off the summer's death. 'I want to be engulfed in you, narrow life,' cries Douve. 'Empty lightning, run on my lips, pierce me!

I love blinding myself, surrendering myself to the earth. I love no longer knowing what cold teeth possess me.'

II

All one night I dreamed you fibrous, Douve, the better to offer you to flame. And green statue wed by bark, the better to rejoice in your glittering head.

Feeling beneath my fingers the dispute of lips and the embers: I could see you smiling at me. And this broad day in you of the coals, blinding me.

III

'Look at me, look at me, I ran!'

I am near you, Douve, I light your way. Nothing between us but this stony lamp, this stilled shadow, our hands the shadow takes. Startled salamander, you do not move.

Having lived that instant when the nearest flesh turns knowledge.

IV

Ainsi restions-nous éveillés au sommet de la nuit de l'être. Un buisson céda.

Rupture secrète, par quel oiseau de sang circulais-tu dans nos ténèbres?

Quelle chambre rejoignais-tu, où s'aggravait l'horreur de l'aube sur les vitres?

IV

Thus we stayed awake, high in the night of being. A thicket gave.

Secret break, by what bird of blood did you pulse through our darkness?

To which room were you returning, where the horror of dawn deepened on the panes?

Quand reparut la salamandre, le soleil
Était déjà très bas sur toute terre,
Les dalles se paraient de ce corps rayonnant.

Et déjà il avait rompu cette dernière
Attache qu'est le cœur que l'on touche dans l'ombre.

Sa blessure créa, paysage rocheux,
Une combe où mourir sous un ciel immobile.
Tourné encor à toutes vitres, son visage
S'illumina de ces vieux arbres où mourir.

When the salamander reappeared, the sun
Was already very low on every land,
The flagstones took on beauty from this radiant body.

And already he had cut that last
Bond which is the heart reached in darkness.

Thus, rocky landscape, his wound opened
A ravine to die in, under a motionless sky.
Still turned toward the windows, his face
Lighted with those old trees where he could die.

Cassandre, dira-t-il, mains désertes et peintes,
Regard puisé plus bas que tout regard épris,
Accueille dans tes mains, sauve dans leur étreinte
Ma tête déjà morte où le temps se détruit.

L'Idée me vient que je suis pur et je demeure
Dans la haute maison dont je m'étais enfui.
Oh pour que tout soit simple aux rives où je meure
Resserre entre mes doigts le seul livre et le prix.

Lisse-moi, farde-moi. Colore mon absence.
Désœuvre ce regard qui méconnaît la nuit.
Couche sur moi les plis d'un durable silence,
Éteins avec la lampe une terre d'oubli.

Cassandra, he will say, hands empty and painted,
Gaze drawn up from lower than any gaze of love,
Take in your hands, save in their embrace
This head now dead where time is ruins.

The Idea grows in me that I am pure and live
In the high house from which I had fled.
Oh that all be simple on the shores where I die
Press into my fingers the book, the obolus.

Smooth me, anoint me. Dye my absence.
Shut down these eyes not acknowledging night.
Bed me in folds of a lasting silence,
Put out with the lamp a land of oblivion.

Justice

Mais toi, mais le désert! étends plus bas
Tes nappes ténébreuses.
Insinue dans ce cœur pour qu'il ne cesse pas
Ton silence comme une cause fabuleuse.

Viens. Ici s'interrompt une pensée,
Ici n'a plus de route un beau pays.
Avance sur le bord de cette aube glacée
Que te donne en partage un soleil ennemi.

Et chante. C'est pleurer deux fois ce que tu pleures
Si tu oses chanter par grand refus.
Souris, et chante. Il a besoin que tu demeures,
Sombre lumière, sur les eaux de ce qu'il fut.

Justice

But you, but the desert! Spread lower
Your gloomy folds of sand.
Wind into this heart so that it will not stop
Your silence like a legendary cause.

Come. Here a thought breaks off,
Here a beautiful country runs out of roads.
Move out on the rim of that frozen dawn
Which yields as your due a hostile sun.

And sing. You mourn twice over what you mourn
If you dare to sing, denying night.
Smile, and sing. He needs your presence,
Dark light, on the waters of what he was.

Je prendrai dans mes mains ta face morte. Je la coucherai dans son froid. Je ferai de mes mains sur ton corps immobile la toilette inutile des morts.

I will take your dead face into my hands. I will lay it out in its coldness. With my hands I will make on your motionless body the useless dressing of the dead.

L'orangerie sera ta résidence.
Sur la table dressée dans une autre lumière
Tu coucheras ton cœur.
Ta face prendra feu, chassant à travers branches.

Douve sera ton nom au loin parmi les pierres,
Douve profonde et noire,
Eau basse irréductible où l'effort se perdra.

The orangery shall be your dwelling-place.
On the table set up in another light
You shall lay down your heart.
Your face shall take fire, riding through branches.

Douve shall be your name far off among the stones,
Douve deep and black,
Irreducible low water where effort shall spend itself.

Vérité

Ainsi jusqu'à la mort, visages réunis,
Gestes gauches du cœur sur le corps retrouvé,
Et sur lequel tu meurs, absolue vérité,
Ce corps abandonné à tes mains affaiblies.

L'odeur du sang sera ce bien que tu cherchais,
Bien frugal rayonnant sur une orangerie.
Le soleil tournera, de sa vive agonie
Illuminant le lieu où tout fut dévoilé.

Truth

Thus until death, faces reunited,
The heart's clumsy gestures on the repossessed body,
Upon which you fade, absolute truth,
This body given over into your weakening hands.

The smell of blood shall be the good you sought,
Frugal good shining on an orangery.
The sun will turn, in its bright agony
Lighting the place where all was revealed.

Tu as pris une lampe et tu ouvres la porte,
Que faire d'une lampe, il pleut, le jour se lève.

You took up a lamp and now you open the door,
What use is a lamp, it is raining, the day breaks.

VRAI LIEU
TRUE PLACE

Qu'une place soit faite à celui qui approche,
Personnage ayant froid et privé de maison.

Personnage tenté par le bruit d'une lampe,
Par le seuil éclairé d'une seule maison.

Et s'il reste recru d'angoisse et de fatigue,
Qu'on redise pour lui les mots de guérison.

Que faut-il à ce cœur qui n'était que silence,
Sinon des mots qui soient le signe et l'oraison,

Et comme un peu de feu soudain la nuit,
Et la table entrevue d'une pauvre maison?

Let a place be made for the one who approaches,
He who is cold and has no home.

He who is tempted by the sound of a lamp,
By the bright threshold of only this house.

And if he stays overcome with anguish and fatigue,
Let be uttered for him the healing words.

What needs this heart which was only silence,
But words which are both sign and litany,

And like a sudden bit of fire at night,
Or the table, glimpsed in a poor man's house?

Chapelle Brancacci

Veilleuse de la nuit de janvier sur les dalles,
Comme nous avions dit que tout ne mourrait pas!
J'entendais plus avant dans une ombre semblable
Un pas de chaque soir qui descend vers la mer.

Ce que je tiens serré n'est peut-être qu'une ombre,
Mais sache y distinguer un visage éternel.
Ainsi avions-nous pris vers des fresques obscures
Le vain chemin des rues impures de l'hiver.

Brancacci Chapel

Candle of the January night on the flagstones,
When we had said not everything would die!
I could hear further off among like shadows
A step which each evening goes down to the sea.

What I cling to is perhaps but a shadow,
But see how it turns you an eternal face!
So had we taken toward darkened frescoes
The futile path of winter's muddy streets.

Lieu du Combat

I

Voici défait le chevalier de deuil.
Comme il gardait une source, voici
Que je m'éveille et c'est par la grâce des arbres
Et dans le bruit des eaux, songe qui se poursuit.

Il se tait. Son visage est celui que je cherche
Sur toutes sources ou falaises, frère mort.
Visage d'une nuit vaincue, et qui se penche
Sur l'aube de l'épaule déchirée.

Il se tait. Que peut dire au terme du combat
Celui qui fut vaincu par probante parole?
Il tourne vers le sol sa face démunie,
Mourir est son seul cri, de vrai apaisement.

II

Mais pleure-t-il sur une source plus
Profonde et fleurit-il, dahlia des morts
Sur le parvis des eaux terreuses de novembre
Qui poussent jusqu'à nous le bruit du monde mort?

Il me semble, penché sur l'aube difficile
De ce jour qui m'est dû et que j'ai reconquis,
Que j'entends sangloter l'éternelle présence
De mon démon secret jamais enseveli.

Ô tu reparaîtras, rivage de ma force!
Mais que ce soit malgré ce jour qui me conduit.
Ombres, vous n'êtes plus. Si l'ombre doit renaître
Ce sera dans la nuit et par la nuit.

Place of Battle

I

Here the knight of mourning is defeated.
As he was guarding a spring, now
I awaken, by the grace of trees
Amid the noise of waters, dream renewing itself.

He says nothing. His is the face I look for
At every spring and cliffside, dead brother.
Face of a vanquished night bending
Over the daybreak of the torn shoulder.

He says nothing. What could he say now the battle is over,
He who was beaten by a word of truth?
He turns his helpless face to the ground,
To die is his one cry, of true repose.

II

But does he weep over a deeper
Spring and does he flower, dahlia of the dead,
At the gates of November's muddy waters
Which bear to us the sound of the dead world?

It seems, as I bend to the arduous dawn
Of this day which is owed me and I won back,
That I hear sobbing the eternal presence
Of my secret demon who was never buried.

You shall surge up, shore of my strength!
But may it be despite this daylight leading me.
Shadows, you are no more. If the dark must be reborn
It will be in the night and by the night.

Lieu de la Salamandre

La salamandre surprise s'immobilise
Et feint la mort.
Tel est le premier pas de la conscience dans les pierres,
Le mythe le plus pur,
Un grand feu traversé, qui est esprit.

La salamandre était à mi-hauteur
Du mur, dans la clarté de nos fenêtres.
Son regard n'était qu'une pierre,
Mais je voyais son cœur battre éternel.

Ô ma complice et ma pensée, allégorie
De tout ce qui est pur,
Que j'aime qui resserre ainsi dans son silence
La seule force de joie.

Que j'aime qui s'accorde aux astres par l'inerte
Masse de tout son corps,
Que j'aime qui attend l'heure de sa victoire,
Et qui retient son souffle et tient au sol.

Place of the Salamander

The startled salamander freezes
And feigns death.
This is the first step of consciousness among the stones,
The purest myth,
A great fire passed through, which is spirit.

The salamander was halfway up
The wall, in the light from our windows.
Its gaze was merely a stone,
But I saw its heart beat eternal.

O my accomplice and my thought, allegory
Of all that is pure,
How I love that which clasps to its silence thus
The single force of joy.

How I love that which gives itself to the stars by the inert
Mass of its whole body,
How I love that which awaits the hour of its victory
And holds its breath and clings to the ground.

Vrai Lieu du Cerf

Un dernier cerf se perdant
Parmi les arbres,
Le sable retentira
Du pas d'obscurs arrivants.

Dans la maison traversé
Du bruit des vois,
L'alcool du jour déclinant
Se répandra sur les dalles.

Le cerf qu'on a cru retrait
Soudain s'évade.
Je pressens que ce jour a fait
Votre poursuite inutile.

True Place of the Stag

A last stag vanishing
Among the trees,
The sand will reverberate
With the tread of dark visitants.

In the house crossed
By the sound of voices,
The alcohol of the declining day
Will spill out on the stones.

The stag we thought surrounded
Suddenly breaks free.
I begin to see that this day has made
Your pursuit vain.

Le jour franchit le soir, il gagnera
Sur la nuit quotidienne.
Ô notre force et notre gloire, pourrez-vous
Trouer la muraille des morts?

Day breaks over evening, it shall sweep beyond
The daily night.
O our strength and our glory, will you be able
To pierce the rampart of the dead?

Bloodaxe Contemporary French Poets

Series Editors: **Timothy Mathews & Michael Worton**

FRENCH-ENGLISH BILINGUAL EDITIONS

1: **Yves Bonnefoy:** *On the Motion and Immobility of Douve / Du mouvement et de l'immobilité de Douve*
Translated by Galway Kinnell. Introduction by Timothy Mathews.

2: **René Char:** *The Dawn Breakers / Les Matinaux*
Translated & introduced by Michael Worton.

3: **Henri Michaux:** *Spaced, Displaced / Déplacements Dégagements*
Translated by David & Helen Constantine. Introduction by Peter Broome.

FORTHCOMING:

4: **Aimé Césaire:** *Notebook of a Return to My Native Land / Cahier d'un retour au pays natal*
Translated by Mireille Rosello & Annie Pritchard.
Introduction by Mireille Rosello.

5: **Philippe Jaccottet:** *Pensées sous les nuages / Cloud Thoughts*
Translated by David Constantine & Mark Treharne.
Introduction by Mark Treharne.

6: **Anne Hébert:** *The Tomb of the Kings / Le tombeau des rois*
Translated by Joanne Collie & Anne Hébert.
Introduction by Joanne Collie.

Other books planned for the series include works by Jacques Dupin, André Frénaud, Guillevic, Pierre-Jean Jouve, Gérard Macé.

BLOODAXE CONTEMPORARY FRENCH POETS: 2

RENÉ CHAR
The Dawn Breakers:
Les Matinaux
Edited & translated by Michael Worton

René Char (1907-88) is generally regarded as one of the most important modern French poets. Admired by Heidegger for the profundity of his poetic philosophy, he was also a hero of the French Resistance and in the 1960s a militant anti-nuclear protester.

Associated with the Surrealist movement for several years and a close friend of many painters – notably Braque, Giacometti and Picasso – he wrote poetry which miraculously, often challengingly, confronts the major 20th century moral, political and artistic concerns with a simplicity of vision and expression that owes much to the poet-philosophers of ancient Greece.

Les Matinaux (1947-49) is perhaps his greatest collection. Published after the War, it looks forward to a better and freer world, whilst also bearing the marks of a deep-seated hatred of all fascisms. It contains some of the most beautiful love poems ever written in French.

Michael Worton's translations convey the essence of Char's poetry (which says difficult things in a simple, traditional way), and his introduction suggests why Char is one of the vital voices of our age.

BLOODAXE CONTEMPORARY FRENCH POETS: 3

HENRI MICHAUX
Spaced, Displaced:
Déplacements Dégagements

Translated by David & Helen Constantine. Introduction by Peter Broome.

Henri Michaux (1899-1984) is one of the notable travellers of modern French poetry: not only to the Amazon and the Far East, but into the strange hinterland of his own inner space, the surprises and shocks of which he has never ceased to explore as a foreign country in their own right, and a language to be learned. Fired by the same explorer's appetite, he has delved into the realm of mescaline and other drugs, and his wartime poetry, part of a private "resistance" movement of extraordinary density and energy, has advertised his view of the poetic act as a form of exorcism.

His insatiable thirst for new artistic expressions of himself made him one of the most aggressive and disquieting of contemporary French painters. If he is close to anyone, it is to Klee and Pollock, but he was as much inspired by Oriental graphic arts.

Déplacements Dégagements (1985) has all the hallmarks of Michaux's most dynamic work: poetry testing itself dangerously at the frontiers, acutely analytical, linguistically versatile and full of surprising insights into previously undiscovered movements of the mind.

David Constantine is Fellow in German at the Queen's College, Oxford. He has published four books of poems and a novel with Bloodaxe, and has translated poetry from French, Greek and German. **Helen Constantine** has taught French at schools and polytechnics in Durham and Oxford. **Peter Broome** is Reader in French at Queen's University, Belfast. He is co-author of *The Appreciation of Modern French Poetry* and *An Anthology of Modern French Poetry* (CUP, 1976), and author of monographs on Michaux and Frénaud.

Other French Editions from Bloodaxe

JACQUES DUPIN
Selected Poems
Translated by Paul Auster, Stephen Romer & David Shapiro

Jacques Dupin was born in 1927 in Privas in the Ardèche. Images of the harsh mineral nakedness of his native countryside run through the whole of his work and figure a fundamental existential nakedness. Dupin is an ascetic who likes the bare and the simple. His poetry is sad, wise and relentlessly honest. He speaks in our ear, as if at once close and far off, to tell us what we knew: 'Neither passion nor possession'.

He is a poet and art critic, and a formidable authority on the work of Miró and Giacometti. This edition of his prose poems and lyrics has been selected by Paul Auster from seven collections published between 1958 and 1982, culminating in his *Songs of Rescue*. It has an introduction by Mary Ann Caws, Professor of French at City University of New York.

PIERRE REVERDY
Selected Poems
Translated by John Ashbery, Mary Ann Caws & Patricia Terry
Edited by Timothy Bent & Germaine Brée

Pierre Reverdy (1889-1960) is one of the greatest and most influential figures in modern French poetry. He founded the journal *Nord-Sud* with Max Jacob and Guillaume Apollinaire, which drew together the first Surrealists. Associated with painters such as Picasso, Gris and Braque, he has been called a Cubist poet, for conventional structure is eliminated in his *poésie brut* ('raw poetry'), much as the painters cut away surface appearance to bring through the underlying forms. But Reverdy went beyond Cubist desolation to express a profound spiritual doubt and his sense of a mystery in the universe forever beyond his understanding.

André Breton hailed him in the first Surrealist Manifesto as 'the greatest poet of the time'. Louis Aragon said that for Breton, Soupault, Éluard and himself, Reverdy was 'our immediate elder, the exemplary poet'.

JEAN TARDIEU
The River Underground:
Selected Poems & Prose
Translated by David Kelley

Jean Tardieu's poetry has an almost child-like simplicity, and in France his work is studied both in universities and in primary schools. Yet while he is a household name in France and has been translated into most European languages, his poetry remains little known in the English-speaking world, despite its immediacy and sense of fun.

Tardieu was born in 1903, and this selection spans 80 years of his writing. In his early years the difficulties of writing lyric poetry in a schizophrenic age led him to a multiplication of poetic voices, and so to working for the stage, and he was writing what was subsequently dubbed 'Theatre of the Absurd' before Beckett's and Ionesco's plays had ever been performed.

This selection includes the sequence *Space and the Flute* (1958), which Tardieu wrote for drawings by his friend Pablo Picasso. Their poems and drawings are reproduced together in this edition.

ALISTAIR ELLIOT
French Love Poems
Poetry Book Society Recommended Translation

French Love Poems is about the kinds of love that puzzle, delight and afflict us throughout our lives, from going on walks with an attractive cousin before Sunday dinner (Nerval) to indulging a granddaughter (Hugo). On the way there's the first yes from lips we love (Verlaine), a sky full of stars reflected fatally in Cleopatra's eyes (Heredia), lying awake waiting for your lover (Valéry), and the defeated toys of dead children (Gautier).

The selection covers five centuries, from Ronsard to Valéry. Other poets represented include Baudelaire, Mallarmé, Rimbaud, La Fontaine, Laforgue and Leconte de Lisle. The 35 poems, chosen by Alistair Elliot, are printed opposite his own highly skilful verse translations. There are also helpful notes on French verse technique and on points of obscurity. This is Alistair Elliot's third book of verse translation, following his editions of Verlaine's *Femmes/Hombres* (Anvil) and Heine's *The Lazarus Poems* (MidNAG/Carcanet).